Simply Ing

HELEN NELLIE

As told to **MARGARET O'BRIEN**

Magabala Books

First published 2018
by Magabala Books Aboriginal Corporation, Broome, Western Australia
Website: www.magabala.com Email: sales@magabala.com

Magabala Books is supported by the Commonwealth Government through the Australia Council, and the State of Western Australia through the Department of Local Government, Sport and Cultural Industries. Magabala Books would like to acknowledge the generous support of the Shire of Broome, Western Australia.

Typeset in 11/16 pt Dante MT by Post Pre-Press
Printed in Australia by Griffin Press Pty Ltd

Cataloguing-in-Publication Data available from
the National Library of Australia

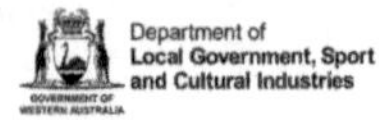

'In order to write about life, first you must live it.'

Ernest Hemingway

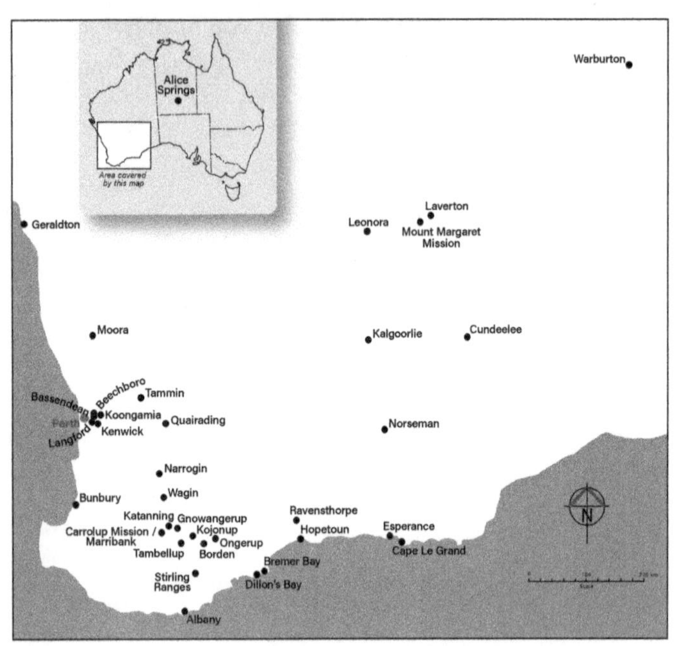
Alice Springs
Area covered by this map
Warburton
Geraldton
Laverton
Leonora
Mount Margaret Mission
Moora
Kalgoorlie
Cundeelee
Beechboro
Tammin
Bassendean
Koongamia
Quairading
Perth
Langford
Kenwick
Norseman
Narrogin
Wagin
Bunbury
Katanning
Gnowangerup
Ravensthorpe
Hopetoun
Carrolup Mission / Marribank
Kojonup
Ongerup
Tambellup
Borden
Esperance
Cape Le Grand
Bremer Bay
Dillon's Bay
Stirling Ranges
Albany
N

This book is dedicated to my mother and father, Tilda and George Nellie, who were forced to live in a world they didn't know. To Auntie Ellie, who helped me to be born and who gave me her name. To my treasured brother and soul mate, Russell Nellie and my darling baby sister, Hilary Nellie. To my precious sons, Harry John and Anthony. And to my Uncle Malcolm Roberts and all the old people who taught me how to be Noongar again.

Contents

Special Thanks

SPECIAL THANKS TO John Van der Giezen, Aboriginal Mental Health Services, for sharing his knowledge of Aboriginal Lore and the Noongar language. To David Bryant, Deputy Principal, and Jacqui Spurling, Aboriginal Language (Wangkatja) teacher, Kalgoorlie-Boulder Community High School, for their assistance with Wongi words. To Henry (Hank) Kordas for his contemporary photographs of Ing. To the Battye Library, State Library of Western Australia for photographic images of the Gnowangerup Mission. To my editor, Bruce Sims, for pulling this book together and Magabala Books for publishing it. To Kim Scott for helping with the manuscript. To the love of my life, my husband, Ron Hall, for his encouragement. And to my sister I adopted, Margaret O'Brien, a special part of me. Thank you for helping me tell my story.

Foreword by Kim Scott

Kaya, nitja kwop nyoondok nitja Noongar maya
waangkiny kaaditj-djinanginy yey.
(hello, it's good you are reading this Noongar language now.)

Nyoondok ngan moort dalangingy,
ngaalang daaliny dalanginy.
You're following my family, following our tongue.

Yoowarl koorl.
Come this way.

DANCING! THAT'S MY fondest memory of Mrs Helen Hall (nee Nellie), or 'Ing' as many know her. Dancing, even though she's a granny; dancing in front of a hundred or more people, then lifting her arms into the air so that they all rise to their feet and shuffle about, squirming and clapping their hands self-consciously. They love it, can't stop grinning. Up to that moment I would never have thought that Auntie

Ing, who is usually so shy in public and would tremble at the very thought of public-speaking, would be commanding a large roomful of teachers like this.

Auntie Ing – simply, Ing – is warm and generous and welcoming, with lots of love to give. She is shy in the company of outsiders. Quiet, but prone to ferocious outbursts of passion. She chuckles a lot.

Ing is complex, in the way of some of the best people. And this is a book written by, and about, one of the best people.

Kayang Hazel Brown introduced me to Auntie Ing in the early 1990s, along with Ryan and Edward Brown, Lomas and Cedric and Lenny Roberts and their sister, Audrey Brown . . . Kayang Hazel had me understand that these were all important Wirlomin people and Auntie Ing, along with her brother Russell, was among them.

'Mission Mob' is the caption on one of her favoured photos: Albert Knapp, Louise Williams, Bobby Woods, Joyce Cockles, Russell Nelly . . . There were others, I can't remember them all and so don't give all the names, but Ing is certainly there. She is, as I remember, at the very centre. One of the Wirlomin, but one of the 'Mission Mob' too, Ing has too many affiliations to fit in a foreword, as you'll see when you read this book.

Another photo she showed me one time: herself, her brother Russell, and their parents George and Matilda (nee Roberts) Nelly. Ing is a very young child, a toddler; Russell still a babe-in-arms. Imagine it as on a movie screen, large and close-up. The photo trembles in Ing's shaking hand, her thumb holding it firmly at its corner. It is bent and creased, that photo, and pock-marked where the emulsion has peeled away.

It must've been soon after that photo was taken that George Nellie and Matilda Roberts were killed in that car crash.

Ing and her brother were very close, although each of them had that passion that sometimes builds a wall and creates a bounce all of its own.

You will read of this in *Simply Ing* and of a life lived as an Aboriginal person, predominately in Western Australia's Great Southern, and the harsh history which split people asunder and isolated them in a racist structure and no real support. Ing makes light of this, so I too will refrain. You can read of that context in a seminal work like Anna Haebich's *For Their Own Good* and many other life stories.

While you're reading, Ing might be playing the piano, if there's one available. There rarely is in a Noongar household, but I've seen Auntie Ing walk into a dusty, community hall and introduce herself to some neglected upright piano. She'll put herself before it, spread her arms wide and begin to play.

She worked at a hostel more than once, preparing meals and catering to groups of young men and women. I've seen the devotion she outlays at such times, tasted it.

One time a niece was stranded by her angry partner, left to herself with no board or bread. In tears, the niece rang Ing, who told her to wait at the railway station and set off to rescue her. It takes more than an hour for the poor woman to get across our city, and her worry and frustration must've built up a good head of steam. She was the one who burst first from the railway carriage doors as the train came to a halt, but there was no hysteria; calm and reassuring, she bundled the young woman up and took her back to home and sanctuary. She whispered comfort to her.

Sweet words. Sweet whispered words abound in Ing, Simply Ing.

Auntie Ing has been very important to the Wirlomin Noongar Language and Stories project. She lamented her loss of her ancestral Noongar tongue, said she couldn't speak it, but her tongue has moved to enough Noongar and Wongi language in her lifetime, and it must've been some form of muscle memory that helped return the sound to us.

The first time we began on one of her father's stories retrieved from the archives it was upsetting for her. Perhaps that was merely the shock of the reconnection, and why not? Here were her father's words from beyond the grave, in this ancient tongue. She stepped back initially, but later led us back to *Dwoort Baal Kaat,* that story of hunting dogs being transformed into seals on the south coast of Western Australia, at that very ocean edge of the Great Southern.

This other story, *Simply Ing,* comes from there too and pulls together secrets and fragments and sweet words to tell of a rich life.

Kim Scott
Professor of Writing
Curtin University

October 20 2017

Introduction

HELLO. MY NAME is Ing and I am a Wirlomin Noongar. I hope you can understand this book by the time I finish. We had such a good time putting it down together, my dear friend and I. So let's begin our travels. Come with me back to the old days. They were beautiful.

1

Early life on the Borden Aboriginal Reserve

THERE'S A LITTLE town of Borden down the southwest of Western Australia, going towards Albany and that's where I was born, in a little mia mia,[1] on July 18, 1947. It's beautiful down there because it has the colour of the Stirling Ranges. Back then, when I was born, it was thick with beautiful bushes. I didn't know nothing about where I was, I just enjoyed the bush life with my mother and my father and my family.

My Auntie Ellie, my mother's eldest sister, delivered me and I was named, my real name Ellie Nellie, after my Auntie.

1 A glossary of words, places and names is included at the end of the book.

And I didn't know until years later that I had my name changed. When I went into the Gnowangerup Mission, the Mission people changed my name and that's how I came to be Helen. But the real name on the Native Welfare list is Ellie Nellie. And that's me. That was sad there because I knew who I was. Mum and Dad called me Ing. Ing means spoilt. I used to be very spoilt – and I never lost my sense of spoiltness. I used to get what I want because I was a very sickly little girl.

Uncle Malcolm, my mother's brother, he was the one that told me I was very sickly when I was born. I nearly died. They had no Noongar doctor, only herbs and things from the trees and roots to dig down, pull up and eat that. They was frightened of the white doctors. They thought they was different people – from out of this world. When any little kids used to be sick you see all them old fellas sitting together, head down. Bush medicine boss. Don't know what it was they had, but it was like a bond that held us all together and that love went from out of their hands somehow into our little bodies and pulled us through, fixed us up. They had the touch. Oh, it was a beautiful touch when they rubbed us down with eucalyptus oil and that. It was old-time oils and it had a different smell to nowadays ones. They make it on their own. I grew up on that. Fixed me. I'm a real believer in that. Old Noongar medicines was very strong, but sometimes, new sicknesses that Noongars never had before wadjala came was too powerful. Our bodies couldn't deal with them new diseases. Didn't know anything about medicine: didn't like the taste of it.

I don't remember much about Borden, but I remember the good times. There was a lot of Noongars there then and we was all sort of like one big family. We lived in a kornt in a thicket of bush at the back of Borden. There was my first cousins, my brothers and their wives or their girlfriends and mums and dads. There was one, two, three, four tent camps. We was like gypsies, Noongar gypsies. We was all together. We didn't have much then; them days we just made things happen when we needed to, because we was always moving about on the farms where Dad worked. Dad was a rouse-about doing fencing and pulling poison weeds up. Orange weeds. Lit fires to burn the weeds. We moved around when Dad was working on the farms. We lived in big sheds with four other families, all sort of like one big clan.

When Dad got rabbits and things, the boys come back, they'll share it up with everybody there on that Borden reserve stomping ground. Rabbits, kangaroos, ducks and that. Ladies would skin them. They was Noongar ways. We were always there, all our family together all the time, the aunties, the uncles, their families, all their children. Their children was older than me; they was in their early teens. My old Auntie Ellie, she was an old doctor lady. Powerful. Very powerful. She was my namesake. She gave me that name, Ellie. She was solid; she used to make the best dampers and that. I used to call all my old aunties and that; I call them Old Mummies. And they used to say, 'Ah, she shouting again. Hurry up, get that meat for her or give her a piece of damper and shut her up.' You didn't need much. Plus the old bush medicine they got. I remember the oldies used to make tea out of eucalyptus and lemon. That was the best tea anybody can ever have. And you can taste that, something like Vicks – better than Vicks. Put it all over. When they burn the eucalyptus they put it on our chest and the fuels of it goes right into our little bodies. Next day you can run for miles, not run out of breath.

Bobtail was the delicacy of the bush for us, but it had to be cooked in a special way. My two cousins, how they cooked it the old way. They pinched them behind the front legs and then down near the back legs; poke them with a stick so all the gas can come out. Then you pull the tail and right at the throat when he dead and gone and that used to bring the guts out. That quick! He got a cross there, pretty little cross, like a pearl, and I used to make beads out of it. That'd be lovely to do, but I'm not going to kill them for that. And the big boys used to get them and kill them, but they did it the Noongar way, save a leg for us, or a tail. The tail, well that's all I had for my teeth to come through. A bobtail tail, that was solid. We usually go for that. I can still taste it. Chew on that. No worries about teeth or dentist or anything. Stick it in honey; suck on that, chew it. Old bobtail, munch on that tail and that would make any little Noongar kids teeth come through strong. Beautiful! Different kind of medicine.

Years later, I give my son, Anthony, that plenty times, put him off to sleep, munch on it. He look around for that bobtail tail first and then he'll eat that. He hardly had biscuits, maybe milk arrowroot. We caught a couple in Kenwick. They were strange, but they were yoorn, bobtail, and that was the loveliest feed. Too nice. That's the last bobtail I ever ate. I never used to like damper, and that was the main thing. Damper and yongka – kangaroo. And eww, I used to hate that kangaroo!

We used to have a lovely feed on sugar ants. Find them all around the bush. Their bodies are big and swollen, with a little white fluffy bundle on their backs, looks like fairy floss on top of it, and it used to taste lovely and sweet. We used to pick them off the ants and have a good feed. That was beautiful. Wasn't much, but so sweet. And ahh, bardi grubs, we used to eat them and all. Delicacy there. Every time wattle come out, yellow wattle trees, you see all the old girls dig right down – well they do that all over Australia, black people, you know – we used to have our way of doing it. They used to get all the roots out way down the bottom and this fat bardi grub was, ahh, talk about beautiful! Buttery taste it had. Kids'd help dig them up. Then you warm it on the side of the fire and it tastes so lovely. They taste like, hmm, bardi grubs. Crunch! And it was too good. Old girls'd have them all in their dresses and skirts and we'd just run along picking them out of their skirts. Hand used to come out and swat at us, 'Go 'way.' Not me, though. I used to pick whatever I want. 'No, she cheating,' other didjas would say. 'She cheating; taking the best ones.' Old girls, they say, 'Now watch these kids so they don't swallow them all.' But you look back now – no way in the world.

We saw the prettiest birds; heard rosellas, little willie wagtails, blue wrens, robin redbreasts and emus. Saw snakes all the time. Tiger snakes, western brown, he was the boss in Gnowangerup and Borden. They used to come in the camp. We was warned, 'Wara, wara, someone after your blood,' if it was cheeky. It was an old saying them days. You see a snake go in front of you, someone after your blood. Bad things. If he didn't cross our paths it was okay, he was looking after us, but if they cross the other side, be very careful. But Uncle Malcolm said, 'No, not like that, you got to be tormenting them for them to get cheeky. Don't go near them when they mating. Old redback, he'll run after you, crawl behind you and the wife will chase you.' Big black one with a red tummy. Very pretty skin but you don't want to get too close, and hot weather they'd be mating. Old tiger, he goes straight up and you better have running shoes on. Some of the boys, I used to see them make belts. They was beautiful. That's what they make stockwhips out of. Got a real click in it when they flick it. That's how they used to do things. Sell them for up to a hundred dollars.

Snakes was everywhere in the bush. They used to love a woman's breast after they had a baby. Main tucker for them. Back in Borden my cousin, she was lying back feeding her boy. She thought that she could feel him sucking on this titty. When she looked she couldn't do nothing, because there was a big snake, lying back like a little baby sucking on the tit, very happy. She froze. She can't do nothing until he turned around and go outside. He was full as anything. She was paralysed; she couldn't move. He didn't bite her or nothing. He just had a good feed of this titty milk.

My mother's Mum and Dad was Dab, from Esperance and Norseman, Warburton. Mighty family that one. They was warriors. They might have seen me when I was a little girl, but I never knew them. I was too small. They used to come and stay with us in Borden. My mother's name was Tilda Roberts and she was Noongar. My grandfather's name was Dab. Mum was the youngest of the Roberts gang. My Auntie, my mother's sister and her husband, he was a big giant of a man. And he was Simon, but his Noongar name was Welbur. Welbur Williams. And my mother's sister was named Ridlan Roberts-Dab. There were lots of Noongars.

My father's name was George Nellie. Dad's father's name was Tony Nellie, and Dad's mother's name was Maggie Winnie. My Dad, he come from up that way somewhere, around other side there, way up on desert mob, Kalgoorlie way. He was Wongi. He was really handsome. In those days them old people must have been very strict with them young boys that grew up there. They drove all young men out of Warburton to go in Alice Springs and go and get themselves wives down south over the years. I think those old people sent him on his way to find a woman down south, pretty nuari girls down south. And that's where he found Mum, somewhere along Hopetoun way.

Dad was a bit of a wag. He was a little short bold fella, but he was strong and he was good looking and he was my brother, Russell's Dad. Russell Nellie, my little brother. I always liked to have my little brother with me. Dad was a good runner and his family was known as wetj – emu. He's the boss. He could run! My father and his brother, my Uncle Bill, they were champion runners. They had a big race from Wagin to Narrogin. I think they won that. They might have something for them in Wagin. So, I was growing up knowing I had a little brother and a Mum and Dad. Mum and Dad was married by Brother Wright in Gnowangerup on June 8, 1954. That's the best part of it, the most wonderful time of my life, knowing they was legally Mr and Mrs George Nellie. That was back then and was the best time in all of my life. That's *my* Mum and *my* Dad. That's where I belong.

My Mum, she was mine and she used to call me *'My little heart'*. The best Mum anyone could ever have. She looked a lot like me. If I could take a photo with an old-fashioned dress on, I think that'd be a photo of Mum. She was my pillow. Pillow of life. I used to just fall on her and go to sleep. Pick me up, cuddle me, put me in bed. I've slept in a lot of beautiful beds, but give me old bushes bed and broom bed. Dad made it like a Slumber King made of shrubs and old hessian waterbags. We jump on it, jump on it, me and my little brother. Mum used to wash them out and stuff them all up with old clothes and make a big woka for us, big rug. And it was the most precious rug I ever had. But that's Dad and Mum. How they used to do it was solid – real spot on. Everything was clean, even when you had nothing. They had these old big boilers and wash them until they was white. And they had that old-fashioned Velvet soap.

We had old bush things. I remember, Russell don't. I was old enough to remember Mum and Dad, both of them. I remember because Dad, he was working, you don't see him most of the day. Mum made everything so comfortable. Big old tent in the kornt on the side for old Uncle and we had the big canvas tent because we were kids. And she used to tuck all the outside up and it was like air-conditioning right through. You got a big bush covering and chuck all the water over it, all around the sides of it and all the old ladies used to come in there, play cards, oh it was like a big old cubby house, lovely and cool. And they had a big old shade. You wouldn't want to live anywhere else. I wouldn't. Comfort.

All the old aunties come there and have tea. Sugar cake I used to love. Old girls make it out of dough and put a little bit of sugar in. You got lolly water there. Turned over and put in the ashes. You got damper, johnnycake and that kangaroo. We never used to eat emu. That's our family, see – wetj. They used to make pudding out of their gadgets inside the kangaroo, instead of throwing it out they make it into a little round pudding, stuff it all up with onion or garlic. Something like a haggis. Like brawn. Oh, you could smell it for miles. Beautiful. I can do that. My old cousin taught me.

Clean, how the old people used to do it, old ladies. Slice it off and you living in luxury. Have a nice little damper on the side. I didn't like kangaroo much, little bit; them days it was all right.

My mother was a very special lady. She was my rock. Mum, she was beautiful. Very shy. I was very shy. My mother used to be very frightened of wadjalas. Shamed. They never had hardly any contact with white people much, but she did gardening for some white farmers. A lot of them old ladies was very frightened of white people. They see a white woman, they'd be gone through the bush. And only fellas that white people would see was old men, and they had to stay put because they were man of the house and they had to look after the woman and the children. Must have been hard for them. Mum used to be that frightened even to talk to wadjalas. She would stand with her head down onto her chest and look away at the ground. I used to be like that when I went into the Mission when I was a little girl. Head down, eyes looking away.

My Dad was a good boxer. He used to train Jackie Dempster in boxing. Used to go to the shows in all the country towns around the southwest. Dad used to put an old sugar bag on his tummy and us kids used to jump on it. He was a tough little man with a big chest. He used to put it on Jackie's tummy or on his back and we used to jump on him, too. Three or four kids used to have to do the weight. That was fun. Used to rub him down with eucalyptus oil.

There wasn't a bloke down there who could beat him. Uncle Ernie Cockle was another boxer, he was boss, a yo-yo; he used to skip around people like Mohammed Ali. He make everybody laugh. Nobody couldn't even see where he was coming from. And he used to hit them big blokes in the front and that bloke started looking around and he'd be behind him till he turned around and then he'll get it, bang! Can't he keep still? Oh, he was boss. Plenty of Noongar boys got a hiding off him when they got too big for their boots.

My friend got me an old newspaper story about Dad when he was boxing.

> The West Australian, Saturday, 24 July 1926:
>
> A full-blooded aboriginal named George Nelly (9.0) quite flabbergasted Godfrey (8.0) during the first round of a five round preliminary, but he lacked science and fought himself to a standstill. At the outset he adopted whirlwind tactics. For a few seconds he vigorously pounded Godfrey who then became very elusive. Godfrey again allowed the aboriginal to chase him round the ring for a while in the second round, and the coloured man tired himself so much that half way through the round he was too feeble to move on his feet or raise his gloves. After the bell went, and Godfrey was walking back to his corner, Nelly waltzed round on one foot and caught Godfrey with a swinging hit to the jaw. The referee had his back turned but it did not matter

> very much for when the gong sounded for the next round the aboriginal was so exhausted he was unable to rise from his chair, and the towel was thrown in.
>
> http://trove.nla.gov.au/newspaper/article/31938473?searchTerm=Aboriginal%20boxer%20George%20Nellie&searchLimits=

Reading that makes me laugh; makes me feel good, like I've found something of me. I'm thinking that'll be him, that's my Dad. He was a funny man, but stubborn. I used to go for a ride with my cousins on horseback, that little Ing person in the front, riding with the boys through the bush, sometimes bareback. Those horses belonged to them but they were kept on the farms. Coming back with a sheep, rabbit fur. I didn't know for a long time what a sock was. My socks was rabbit fur. Dad used to stick them inside my water boots he bought at the old co-op. I was the luckiest person ever. Out of all them little kids I had the warmest feet. They used to reckon, 'You got no socks, only rabbit fur.' I reckon, 'I don't need socks, my Dad made this for me.' They reckon they wish our Dad can do that. And I tell Dad, 'Put some that in there for these fellas.' Yeah, he do it. What we had, well the other kids had to have, too. That's how kind they was, Mum and Dad. They were beautiful, them two. Stick it all together. I don't know how he done it. There must have been the glue in them. They all be pleased. We all got lovely warm foot. And it used to get very cold near the Stirling Ranges. You walk through the field, there used to be ice hanging off the grass.

When I was only three or four years old, we rode on Uncle Malcolm and Uncle Welbur Williams' horse and cart down the back road from Borden to Gnowangerup. Lots of Noongars was there. They lit all the fires. Three or four big fires. And the music, it's still in my head now. They had banjos, ukulele, guitar, piano accordion, little tiny round squeezebox, mouth organ, bottle-top things and the spoons in the beat with the guitar, all them old Noongars. Banjo! My old Uncle Frank was the best. His brother was Paddy Coyne. He could almost make that banjo talk. And they used to dance. That was deadly, just to listen. And beautiful dancers I ever seen in my life. Corroboree was mainly all cut out by then. I used to just sit down quietly and watch – after they told to get me out of the middle. Watch all the old ladies swinging around.

And it was beautiful to watch. Sometimes they pick me up, swing me round with them. Who'd ever thought all my uncles and aunties can do beautiful dancing like that bare foot. Nearly the whole reserve was there. All the Gnowangerup mob used to come there, play two-up. Oh, there was certain ones used to get drunk, make a fool out of themselves, but no one never used to worry about drinking in them days. When they come to these beautiful dances, oh, give me Borden and Gnowangerup any day. Watch all them old people and the band, all these old-time songs. There was Noongar songs, wadjala ones. I can still hear it in my mind now and I can smell the picture of home. They were beautiful days, them days.

They used to have a lot of races, foot races down there too. Stand in line and race each other. See all the old fellas standing with their big beards way down here to their waist, looked like a mob of Father Christmas's only all brown. And it used to look funny, but they were solid runners. Never a dull moment. I had a photo. I don't know where I put it, of Dad in the front, running.

≈

On the reserve was the cutest little whitest dog. He was called Tibby Tibby and he was my favourite. And all the old men long time ago went to dig graves. They get paid for digging the graves. Well, Uncle Andy Coyne, Uncle Frank Coyne and Dad, all there in this Gnowangerup cemetery digging this grave. It was dark, after the sun went down and not so hot. So, my Dad and Uncle Andy, they digging away and they look. They could see this white thing standing on the edge of this grave, looking down at them. Old Noongars was the frighteningest people out. They thought it was a ghost, but really it was this fluffy little white dog.

Well, Uncle Frank, when he telling us had cramps laughing because two grave diggers, they was way down six feet. Little short, black, George Nellie, he put one spring and he was standing on top. Uncle Andy was screaming, 'Get me out of here, George!' But, Dad was gone, like a bullet, back to the reserve. Ah, true. And brother Eddie and them, who was out on the road, they reckon when they looked they thought Dad, he was in the races again because he went past them that fast he never looked back, not knowing he was running away from his own dog! That Tibby Tibby dog, he didn't know what they was running for. He thought it was a big game and he's after them, following Uncle Andy and Uncle Frank home. Uncle Andy was going to kill him, but then he felt sorry for him and picked him up and carried him along, back to the reserve. Dad, he wouldn't get out of that camp. Mum couldn't look, she was laughing too much. All the old aunties, they was crying laughing. I didn't know what was going on, I was only a little girl and Russell was a baby. Don't need a drink to have fun when my Dad's around, skipping around 'til he knocked himself out. And from then, them Noongars in Gnowangerup tormented Dad. They tormented him properly.

Dad was a frightened man. Instead of him sleeping in the front, he'd put Mum. And there used to be a lot of weelos in them days. Used to spook us quiet with that call they got. 'Sssshhh,' he'd go and make sure we were quiet – till I got to a stage where I realised what was going on. I used to just sit back and frighten him some times. I'd sneak around the outside of the tent and put a little stick under his bed and jiggle it around just a bit. He was frightened of snakes and jump up, 'Get the broom! Get the broom!' Mum would go, 'What you doing that for, Pooya [her nickname for Dad]?' 'Aaagh, snake here!' But it was only a stick. He felt like killing me and Russell. Ah true. I was the worst. But he never used to hit us. He used to go for the big boys, my cousins if they teased him to get a laugh out of him.

≈

There was these old trees. They had Noongar way of saying them – mungart trees. And mungart trees are really beautiful light green trees. Beautiful smell in the evening. But with the colours of Christmas decorations on it they come up a real picture of a Christmas tree. The old people would hang popcorn, tinsel and streamers on the mungart tree. I remember that was my first true Christmas. All them old mungart trees. They just hung like a willow tree, but pretty green. Sugar tree, jam gum, little gum and it's the sweetest gum I ever tasted. It was like lollies. Mum used to mix them with sugar and sprinkle all the sugar round on them. That was our lollies. No use wondering when you going to go to the toilet. It might be a week after. They usually blocked us up and all, but that was good to have sweet gum.

One time, my Mum and Auntie, they digging, digging for rabbits in a big burrow. Digging and digging. They got way down. Mum was a big fat lady and my Auntie wasn't much behind her. Mum reckon, 'Ah, we got something with fur on the end.' Fur was on the end, all right. A big, fat cat. It jumped clean on top of Mum. And she couldn't shout and the other one couldn't look – she was crying laughing. I was surprised. Didn't know what they laughing at, shouting. I was playing on my own right over, but knew something was there. Thought it was a rabbit. Then I see this big, stupid, orange cat. It just come straight out of the hole, looked at them. Must have thought these two funny people. I just watched the end of the action. It must have been a wild cat or one that strayed away from the farm. Well, they never go far from the farms. I can hear the old girls laughing, 'Where's the rabbit?' I never realised it was that funny until I got older when Uncle Malcolm telling me. That was the good times down in Borden. I still got little bit of things is in my mind, my special memories.

My two nieces, Edna Yorkshire and Clara Yorkshire, they runned away from Gnowangerup Mission, but they always ended up home at Mum and Dad's. We wasn't at the Borden reserve this time, we was at a big farm down south. All the oldies used to go and put fencing down for the bosses. My nieces, they knew where our family was and they come straight there. I knew they were there but no one else did. They was hiding from the old people, but I could pick them girls out of the shadows and kept throwing stones at them, looking at them. I knew they was running away from something. This day I must have got on their nerves, throwing stones and wanting them to piggyback me around and go and see all the old fellas. They said, 'We'll catch her. We'll shut this little girl up.' I didn't know nothing and I went for a piggyback.

In the middle of the farm there was a big stump, like a jarrah tree, big one that farmers cut down. Cousins, they put me on this big tree, up on top of the stump. In that farm was a big lot of pigs. 'Pig, pig, pig, pig, pig,' they singing out as they run back to the fence. I was up there on that stump, safe, pretty safe, but I screamed my head off. They just left me there in the middle of the field, and oh, big pigs, little tiny pigs and all the pretty pigs you could ever see in your life. And they just was all around this tree. Well, the old people on the other side down that hill, they was putting fencing through and they could see me on top of that stump. They knew I was too low [little] to get up on top of the stump; someone had to put me up. That's where they got caught out.

Ahhh, you could see all the old boys come running over with sticks and all, their hands going. 'How she get up there? What you fellas, what do you left this girl on here for? She could have jumped over, then what's going to happen? You would have been belted back to the Mission.' My nieces, they reckon, 'She's a nuisance. She wants us to carry her on our back all the time.' And my old Uncle Malcolm and them, they say, 'No, she's not. You got to get used to her.' They reckon, 'You don't know what she like when she on her own. We pleased you here, she's a little devil on her own.' Then they said to those two nieces, 'Right, you two girls, you going back to the Mission. We taking you back today. You not going to come round here think you can frighten her. She's worse enough to live with now. You going back this afternoon, as soon as we get her off that old trunk.'

Cousins said to me before they was taken back, 'We going to catch you in the Mission when you come there.' 'Not me!' standing there waving them going back to the Mission. They sitting there on that horse and cart, sulky, heads down. Then I even went for a ride, had an ice cream. I was a very spoilt little girl. And they got their last ice cream before they went home to the Mission. And all the oldies singing out, 'Fancy them girls coming here, doing that to her.'

Years later, Edna telling me, 'You was a wicked little girl. Funny, but wicked. First little girl I seen that never was touched. You got away with a lot of things. Never even got a smack.' That's true, because I was sickly little girl – and spoilt. I said, 'You old people make me like that, hmm?' 'Oh, we all had a share, there, but you got away with a lot of things.'

When I was only a little kid, I remember walking along with a brand new dress on. Pretty little dress it was. I can see the little colours in it and all the flowers. Big bow at the back. My little nephew run; he run across the bridge. Me, I was dressed up in my new shoes, socks, first shoes and socks in my life. Felt strange. Little bush kid walking along in shoes and socks. Pretty little dress on, walking across that bridge. My little nephew was in front of me. All of a sudden, I stepped out of the way watching him and I took a lovely little swim in the cold water. Icy cold water coming through from the Stirlings. You could even see ice floating down. Dress was a mess. Where there was supposed to be a ribbon in my hair was a frog! And instead of calling, 'Mummy, quick!' I say, 'Mummy queeetch.' My aunties they sort of looked away. 'Don't, please, you'll start her off.' 'Don't laugh at her, next she'll throw herself in the fire.' I must have been a funny little kid. After, I had to change, but I didn't want to take this pretty dress off. First dress I had. That was a big thing.

That's the last time I can really remember Mum and Dad and all the family together. Don't know where we was going that time, maybe into Gnowangerup for the show. Everyone was welcome. You could see all the boxing. Got on the old diesel train from Borden to Gnowangerup, playing two-up and dancing. They called it the Boronia Diesel. And you could smell boronia in it, too. I remember it was a lovely old train. Not far to go, but that was a ride of the century there, especially when you coming from the bush. Always a smiling face there.

They used to go mad on two-up. I stand there in the middle, looking. They say, 'Get that girl out of the middle.' Every note, that old five-pound notes, ten pounds, I run and pick that notes up, but my Uncle's dog, he beat me. He'd be sitting there looking like that, staring at me, 'Try to take it off me, sister.' He had a monkey face. That was his name, Monkey. He used to see me coming with a little bag, he run and grab the money and look at me, savage way, too. You don't know whether to run or what. Grrr. He never bit us, he used to carry us on his back. Big sort of tall sort of dog. But, in the two-up school he had his job, pick his father's money up. I used to hate that dog.

That was life back then and they took that away from us. There was a nasty old policeman would grab kids and take them to the Mission. Didn't matter what their Mum and Dad said, they just took them.

When my little brother was born, he was tiny little Noongar. I used to pick him up and carry him, him and my nephew in my little dress, skirt pulled up like a cradle, and they used to say to me, 'What you got there Ing? Sand? Chuck that sand away.' And a little blonde head will fall out. He was a little cutie, little jellyfish. And that's when I remember years ago how Mum run, because she'd get very frightened when I carry him around. She wasn't laughing. He was like a little rag doll. Now and then, he'll sit up and look around, lie back down again. 'Look at him, he's just as stupid as her.'

My little brother was healthy, but fat! He was always very fat when he was a little fella. Little blondie. His hair was like golden wattle and he was a little blackfella with this yellow hair. That was the in thing in our family. A lot of our little kids was born like that, blonde hair and black skin. In them days there was a thing called djanak. That means devil. A devil or balyat man that sits in the bush and grabs little fellas. Wadjala was djanak. 'Get hold of him, he's a djanak, that little boy.' And all the old people used to say, 'Watch him, he's got fair hair. Kaanya. Get hold of him. Djanak will catch him.' They used to be that frightened of little blonde-headed kids. 'You watch him, he's going to get a hiding if he keep running around.' No clothes on, little fatty run, leave all the kids behind. First thing you see is the guts coming toward you. Or he be sitting high up on Dad's or one of my uncle's shoulders. I used to call him little bully-headed, bandy-legged Nellie. He'd cry and complain that I was calling him names and try to catch me.

Saying djanak or weelo was going to catch him was Noongar way of telling little kids: 'Shhh, night-time now, time to sleep. Balyat man or djanak be looking at you.' Or, 'Weelo coming,' That's that little bird, he's for Wirlomin mob. He make funny, awful noise, *wee-lo, wee-lo.* That's how we got that company, Wirlomin. It was a sound that it will go right through your brains. 'Lie down now, weelo coming here,' they say to the little kids. Coax little kids away, belt them. And they used to have fires all around the camps, little fires to keep that bird away from us. The bird looked pretty, little long-legged thing, but they could run. And when they want to hide from you they just sit down and you just think it's a branch laying there. It just sits still. If weelo there, you never heard a kid make a noise. They're frightened to even move. Everybody looking, but the only thing moving are these big, brown eyes.

Mum never went to hospital with me, nor my little brother, Russell. You didn't need a hospital in them days. Noongars, they had very clean midwives. Never had luxury sheets. They used to have flour bags, sugar bags – white ones. Boil it up, boil it up, make it into a big sheet. And how they do it till it's pure white, hanging out on the line. All the blankets was clean, especially for babies. And that was just magical. Because that was for all the kids that was born in the camps. Always a big pot there with boiling water. Had to boil it. My Auntie, I got her name, Ellie, she was one of them midwives. Very clean old ladies. You'd think what they used to do, you'd think it was a hospital anyway. When they deliver babies, they always wash their hands. That's how I learnt. But they had their own medicine. It was the beauty of it. I don't know what they done but it was so spotless.

The camp had to be damped all around. And inside, just a lady and her husband, if he wanted to go there. It was a big canvas tent and inside was beautiful and cool if it was hot and wintertime it was warm. What they do with it I don't know. We weren't allowed to be around there. They done what they had to do. Some of the men and women now got families of their own, great grandparents. That was a hospital for us. None of us all been registered, but we got into this world somehow. Ha! Something went right. And that's a treasure of being in Borden and knowing that really happened for all us Noongar kids who went through Borden at that time. Most of them now all grandparents like me. We're still brothers and sisters like from the Mission.

The first Father Christmas I ever seen in my life came to the Borden Reserve. A lot of other little Noongar kids was there, you know, I grew up with. My brother was just a baby then. Everybody hated the looks of this big bloke in red. I must have been about three. And I look up and there's this bloke, all in red. I thought I was looking at the devil! He was the ugliest looking thing out. I hated the looks of him. No one was going to get me there. A white hand came out to take me, picked me up and carried me right to this big old red man. I yelling, 'Nooo!' You know, Noongar words for swearing was terrible. I still know a little bit. They didn't know what I was talking about. If he could understand Noongar words, he'd be that shamed. Yeah, he would have been that shamed.

I cursed Father Christmas with some pretty little Noongar words. No one understood a word what I was saying but I knew every word. He started laughing. I was scared of him because, well, when you come from the bush, you know all the birds, emus, everything in the bush, and then you're faced up with this man. I didn't know what he looked like. He looked like a monkey or a big red something, so I punched him! First person ever to punch Father Christmas. Yeah, little bush girl punch him up and down. Poor old Father Christmas's hat come off. He hardly had any hair 'cause he was bald. Ah, poor old Mr Street. He was that Father Christmas. I think he was glad to get away from me, he must have had scratches down his face, the beard was supposed to be there on his face, it was stuck way over there, halfway round his neck, hat was gone south somewhere. I wouldn't even look at him. Poor old fella, yeah, he was a dear old Dad. Well, I must have made my father and mother that shamed they had to take me home. Mum was saying, 'Shhh, keep her quiet, keep her quiet. Kaanya, kaanya.' They was good times.

Years later Mr Street used to say, 'You're a funny little girl.' That's all he used to say to me, 'Helen, you're a funny little girl.'

2

The one-way truck

ANYWAY, THE NEXT time we come back to the Borden Reserve I remember a big truck coming from Gnowangerup Mission. The Mission was about 25 miles from Borden. Wasn't far. You could almost walk there. Every Easter they'd come and give us rations, food rations and fruit and cakes for the kids. Well, we was pleased to see this big truck full of fruit and my niece sung out, 'Hey Auntie, come for ride.' Yeah! My two nieces was in the Mission before me. I wouldn't go for no one else, only for those two, because we sort of grew up together. Pig ladies. They the ones that put me on that tree stump, call the pigs and leave me there in the middle of that field. They must have had it in for me, payback. So, I jumped on the back of this truck. I hadn't been on a truck before, even a car. Been on a horse and cart. I was that excited. This was the biggest thing ever happened to me. I could see Mum and Dad and I called out, 'Hey, Mummy, Mummy, Daddy, Daddy, look at me. We going for a ride on the truck!' When that truck started driving away, I was laughing and waving. But they wasn't even smiling. When that truck driver knew they had enough of those kids, off to Gnowangerup Mission we went.

It went through the gate. Above the gate was a big wooden sign in the shape of a boomerang – UNITED ABORIGINES MISSION GNOWANGERUP. 'Oooh, look at that!' Little bit of excitement, but I was still looking back to see if Mummy and Daddy was following us. 'Where's Mum and Dad?' They never come. Frightened.

Took me through the gates and into the Mission. Sat down. I can't recall the feelings then, but it was terrible. And oh, the other kids was laughing and giving us lollies and that. I never ate those lollies, I just hold on to them. That stuck in my mind and I still feel shut down when I think about that truck. To think that big truck came and picked me up and I wasn't meant to be with my family anymore.

I must have been about four or five when I went into the Mission the first time. My Mum wasn't well from my little brother. And I'm thinking . . . Well, didn't know what I was thinking them days, I was too young to understand, but there was all of a sudden an emptiness coming over me and I couldn't really understand this emptiness. What they doing to us? When we got to the Mission we stood there looking like lost little lambs that had got away from their mothers. It was a terrible feeling. No, it was bad. Frightening. Didn't know what to do. I can remember that. I was too young to figure out what was going on, but it seemed like a lifetime. But I knew something was wrong and I can't seem to work it out. I just stood there looking at all those people coming over, smiling. 'Hello Ellie, we got a bed for you.' Can't say nothing. Shook my head, put my head down. Can't say nothing. Where Mum and Dad? The other kids was crying by then and I started crying too. Over the years, this part of my life, it's gone. I had to live with it and try to get on but I didn't know how. They put us in the Mission and left us there. Put me in them dormitories and we were stuck there.

We were scrubbed. Had my hair short. I cried all week. Whoever had nits had their hair cut bald nearly. This horrible old soap, it was like a washing soap but you could use it for your hair and they used to scrub that for nits. Ah true, I think no wonder our hair was that shiny; it was through this stupid soap. I hated that soap. Tried to hide it but they find it. I tried all little tricks, all little horrible tricks.

They put that stupid ribbon on my hair. If there was something I hated it was that silly ribbon. It looked quite nice. And I asked: 'What's these things?' 'That's your towel, your little pinafore and thongs for you to wear. A little cup there with toothpaste and brush.' I didn't know how to use it and I got into trouble plenty times over that. Stuff for the teeth, toothpaste, it was more like a lolly than this thing to scrub your teeth. I didn't know nothing about cleaning teeth. I had hardly any teeth when I went in there. They were all rotten from eating sweet stuff and not cleaning my teeth. We ate lollies what Mum and Dad give us, the biscuits, the cool drinks. At the Mission, they taught us how to clean our teeth, but we always had Christmas on that toothpaste. It was lovely. We used to hide them, put it underneath our pillow. They used to come in there and it was all plastered all over the pillows. I was always getting into trouble over that. 'Helen, you done it again!' 'My name not Helen, it's Ellie,' I used to tell them. 'Well, while you're in the Mission your name is Helen.' 'No it's not!' They was stubborn people, but so was I. I used to give cheek back. Got smacked on the hand. 'Stop eating the toothpaste! That's not a lolly. It's for your teeth.' They took us to the dentist in Katanning. I had a lot of teeth pulled out. Years later had more pulled out in Kalgoorlie. Made gold teeth for me.

At first we didn't have shoes, had them brown sandals and odd pairs of socks they had left over from the missionaries' kids. We never used to wear them anyway. Mostly we just run around in bare feet. And that's how it started. I don't recall all of my childhood when I was that small, but I sort of fitted into the Mission life slowly. I had to do it myself. You wanted to hate it, but you can't, because it's the only place you knew after they took us. But way back in the back of my mind I knew my home was Borden. That's where they took me away from Mum and Dad. They, the white people, policemen, they said they wasn't looking after us. But don't know what this Mission got for us. That was the awfullest turning point of my life. I never done nothing wrong to deserve that. All I wanted was Mum and Dad and the Welfare people did things in a terrible way.

I didn't speak much English when I first went into the Mission. We always spoke our Noongar language in the reserve. But, I learnt English. I had to. We weren't allowed to speak our language. I lost all of my Noongar words, most of them. If they caught us talking our language, they'd get us by the hand and *bang bang bang*. Wash our mouths out with old Velvet soap. Scrub it all out, saying they trying to get rid of our language. But we kept it to ourselves. Even when we was that young we had our ways. Picking pegs up on cold mornings in the Mission. We had to pick all them pegs up. Some big girls would just drop them on the ground. And then we talk our language that way and laugh it on our own. We was lucky there. But if a missionary hear about it you'd get the biggest hiding out, banged on the head, or you won't have pudding, or you won't have a fig until tomorrow; until when we got bigger, I think they was frightened to hit us then, when we were starting to grow up into young women.

I used to cry when I had my quiet times. Everything I been Nellie for gone down the drain and issued with a new name. That's a sad part. That's not my name, but they just come in, take things off us and tell us to be thankful for where you are. How can you, when even your own identity is gone. Nothing there. Oh, it was terrible. I missed Mummy.

My mother. I still do now. Dad, yeah, but he was the boss. That's something I think life tried to take away but it will always be there. That's the thing that's really hurting me now. Why they have to do that? They didn't have to do that, have some bit of our old Noongar ways.

We had our own Noongar teacher when I first started at the old Mission school, so my first teacher was my old Uncle, Uncle Clifton Flowers. When I first went into the Mission I wouldn't listen to no white people. They had to nearly strap me to a chair to sit down and listen. He was educated white way. He taught us how to count and how to spell. I was never any good at spelling, still no good, but I learnt enough just to get by. He also taught us some Noongar words when no Mission people was around. I remember how he used to sing them beautiful hymns. I was his pet because I used to do everything right for him. He was my old Uncle. He was a big bloke. He had four children in the Mission of his own, but he was sort of my first teacher in the old Mission church. And we used to go and sit there with him. That was good. He was very brainy for a Noongar man, like a professor. But something went wrong down the years; he just faded away, and he ended up in Claremont. I think it was too much pressure. After that he still knew a lot and we used to ask him lots of things and he used to tell us everything he knew about what he went through, but he didn't teach again. And I respected my old Uncle. I called him Dad.

I learnt to play the piano and the organ and still now remember all the old songs. Never had lessons. I just played by ear. It was lovely. I played Chopsticks at a concert. I learnt how to count. For me that would have been the hardest thing out. I used to hate writing and printing. I'm still the worst speller and trying to spell Noongar and Wongi words is the hardest thing out. I learnt how to sweep a floor. Didn't like mopping the floor much. We didn't know what a mop was for at first. Had dust and dirt floors on the reserve, only wet bags all around. Neat. Very neat. Old people was very clean people. They were beautiful. Looked at this mop. And they said you mop like that and showed us what to do. So we sort of pushed it around as best as we can, had fun, all riding on the back of it. That was good. Fun days. We liked chasing each other with mops. Get into trouble over that. My cousin always in trouble, fighting with the mop. We'd get a good smack sometimes.

We all had our precious toys and things. I had a rabbit sitting on a trough that Dad won for me at the Gnowangerup Show. One of them old clay ones. I also had a rag doll. That's *my* doll. All the kids had dolls. I had a Golliwog made by people who sold them at the show. I loved that Golliwog. He was a funny-looking doll but he was my favourite. I think he was a symbol of myself. He didn't have a name, just Golliwog. I don't know what happened to them, but I know I had a lot of thieves for that Golliwog – lots of kids watching, and I watch their eyes. 'That's *mine*!' Sometimes the boys used to nick it. Later on they get Russell to because they know I wouldn't hit him. Run, chase him down. I think them boys pulled Golliwog's two eyes out, took his little stripy jacket off him and a tie.

I was too sick to go to the show with Mum and Dad. I had measles, mumps and chicken pox all one after the other. Sickly, that's why they called me Ing – spoilt. When we was sick Dr McCormack used to see us. He was a real nasty man. Real prejudiced. I think there was a lot of dislike of him. Didn't like Noongars from the bush, but he tolerated us. Didn't do us any harm. We used to say we get the best treatment off him because we were Mission kids.

One of the first things I ever learnt at the Mission was to ride a bike when I was seven, six. Ride around the Mission on this rusty old two-wheeler bike with big wheels. We had fun on that bike. All the kids had to share that bike. We used to fight over it. I probably pushed all the other kids away. It was taken off us for a week and then if you behave yourself you could ride it again. At first we only had one bike, but I think later on we had one for girls and one for boys. That was the fastest car I ever had, that old bike. Raced the boys and all. Didn't have no brakes. When you going down the hill you like this, 'Aaaaaaggghhh', legs out and all, yelling we can't stop this thing. Straight into the bush, grab hold of a bush and you off the bike. Ah, it was a funny old thing. It was like them wheels knew us, you know, I got to go good for this person. Lots of scrapes and bruises. Foot, knee, elbows. Elbows the worst one.

Birthdays was good. We used to have big birthday parties. Whoever's birthday was in that month they'd have all the kids' party. Boys one side and girls the other, but we was always together and that was fun. We had everything, big cake with candles for the boys and the girls, sing happy birthday, and lovely presents, handkerchief, or jumper, socks, underpants and things, and we thought it was great until we realised there ought to be something better than that. And these little Matchbox toys, brother, I used to fight all them little boys for the cars and push it, 'brrrrmmm', along the ground. And they'd cry, 'We're going to go tell on you, Helen. That's ours! That's a boy's toy, not a girl's toy.' 'Ah, you keep talking, you not getting it back.'

If mothers and fathers was around they was all welcome. All the mothers and all the fathers, grandparents, aunties, uncles, they could come. Our Mission was like that. Later on, I learnt that kids at some of the other missions wasn't allowed to see their Mum and Dad. Wasn't allowed to even talk about them and if their brother or sister was in the Mission, they wasn't allowed to talk to them or play with them. We'd have a big, open-air party, because the big girls used to love cooking. So there was everything on a big, long table, you'd just pick out what you want.

We used to make our own ice cream out of Ideal Milk, cow's milk, gelatine, sugar. And if we wanted to mix some fruit in, we put fruit in it. It was the best ice cream in all the world. Tasted beautiful right down to the end – so fun.

Mr Street used to make it for us. Old Tom his name was. He was that Father Christmas that I punched up. He was the old Superintendent of the Gnowangerup Mission and he was like an old father to us.

Christmas time, oh, that was full of everything. It was real special. The best day of all was Christmas Day. Sneak around in the beds. 'Wonder what she got.' Swap it. Changing all the toys around. And the old lady that used to come there every year, that was our Father Christmas. We all learnt to believe she was Father Christmas, but we knew who she was. We know who Father Christmas is. She just had a dressing gown on and Father Christmas hat, that's all. No beard. She was a beaut old lady, Miss Hipwell. She was a Hipwell all right, because she had a hump sort of back. She already had all the presents written down, which toys was whose. And that's what we didn't know. She reckons: 'You won't be having no toys.' 'What for?' 'You going around swapping all your toys with everybody. I know what I gave you.' We won't see our toys for a month after.

When we got wild with her we used to say, 'Ah, you old witch, you got your black snake.' Strap. If we was naughty we'd get Charlie, that's his name, Charlie. Charlie, the black snake from inside the tyre. She said, 'I'm going to get Charlie.' And that was funny times, because Melva was so funny. She was bigger than me. She'd do things and she'll point at me so I'd get the blame. But I was so innocent. I could throw an innocent face, she can't. I get let off all the time. 'Melva, we are sick and tired of you getting these little girls into trouble.' And she used to get a little smacking. I'd point and laugh at her, 'Ha ha.' Best time, I reckon.

Rona was older than us, used to pull us together. Dolly and me used to sit on her, pull her hair. 'You not with us.' That was cruel and I felt sorry for her. She stuck with us over the years. We used to sit back and have a good laugh when we was drinking in the park. 'Remember what we used to do in the Mission?' She'd say, 'Oh, you two was cruel. I'm not talking to you anymore' and she'd walk off and we'd be sitting back laughing.

We had a beautiful Christmas lunch. All cooked at home. We had everything. Turkeys. They put all the turkeys in the middle, beetroots and roast sweet potato. I used to love baked sweet potato, pumpkin, carrots. We used to have a big garden and all go and do the Christmas picking, fruit and veggies. That was the best time of year for us kids. Mothers and fathers, aunties, uncles, sisters, brothers, cousins, everybody used to come. Take food home to reserve after.

We used to put on concerts at Christmas time. I don't know if I was a shepherd or an angel. I might have been too fat to be an angel, so they had me as one of the shepherds. I fell over the hay and the sheep – real sheep. I think it might have been Old Bob Holland, the sheep. Rolling on the floor, us girls, we couldn't help laughing. We had to go out and they put someone else there until we behave ourselves. And when you do something like that, you looking around at all the other kids and they can't stop laughing, neither could you. We all getting into trouble all at once. They used to call me a troublemaker. Ah, some of the things I used to be up with. Charlie would come out. 'Look out, Helen, Charlie coming.' Oh dear, poor Old Miss Hipwell, God bless her, she's in heaven now. She's still looking after us. She'll be saying: 'Those girls will never learn.'

Every year we went to Bremer Bay for three weeks in the Christmas holidays. I used to love that. All get on top of that big, green Commer truck with wooden sides, same one that took me to the Mission. We had to pack all the things up nice and neat with all our clothes and things and food. I think I would have been six, seven, eight. Little kids get in the bus. Big blue and yellow bus. Had Eagles football club colours. Prettiest bus out. Every Sunday that bus would go around the reserve and pick up all the Noongars, bring them back for church. They wanted to put me in the bus to go to Bremer. 'No, I'm getting up top with all the big kids,' and you sitting way up high on the back of that Commer truck with all the big boys and girls. And you'd see for miles on this big truck, up on top with all the luggage.

It was good fun going to Bremer Bay, Dillon's Bay really, setting up our tents. That was our holiday home. Running around playing with just our bathers on. Getting ready to go for a swim. Whoever helped can go for a swim. Never used to worry about getting sunburnt. That was an evil thing for white kids. We were brought up for this country. Tough skin.

Dillon's Bay had a big sea pool there. All that part was Bremer to us. That was the best time of our lives. We had everything. Not a care in the world. We done everything we could think of. The weather was lovely. You go for walks on that beautiful sandy beach or you could lie outside on the beach, but the water used to come up into the river. They talk about overseas how beautiful is the countryside. Bremer had its own beauty. You'd go out onto the beach and you could see for miles, you could walk for miles, you know never-ending story, walk right around and we knew where we was going. That was our way. You want a fish? Take a little hand line and chuck it in, light a fire and you got a fish. That was good times. Old white people, they were understanding like that. You catch a fish and cook it on the beach. Never even heard nothing about bushfires and that in them days, it was just fun. It was beautiful, absolutely beautiful; great big rocks, but the water would always be icy cold. You'd stand there, not wanting to go into that cold water and some of the boys would come along and push you in. Once you in, you right.

So, some of the bigger boys used to hit that water and you see a salmon coming in. Old people picked certain ones, taught them how to catch fish Noongar way. Saw it once in a while when we was kids. Didn't think much about it. Later saw Uncle Malcolm do it and explain how this happens. Used to wonder why the fish were coming in. But that old ocean was watching us. That old Noongar they call him. When a stranger goes there and he knows you don't belong in that country that sea will get so rough! See that big waves coming in. Wild because there's someone stranger there. Don't know who they is; he can't work them out. Old people used to teach me that's old Noongar. He'll look after you long as you look after him. Powerful. You always had your feed. It was good but you had to carry that big fish all the way home. And Mission people, they say, 'Where you got that from? You kids got no line on you.' Don't say nothing. Don't tell 'em nothing, that's our secret. I used to tell Dolly, 'Don't tell no one.'

We had a big mulberry tree when we went on holidays in Bremer Bay. They reckon it's still there. I'd love to go down there, take my little grannies. Put all your little black clothes on because you're going up that mulberry tree. We was little blackfellas but we were blacker. Red lipstick, red teeth. We had mulberry fights all the time. The boys used to beat us. Get stung by them mulberries and you weren't allowed to cry. 'Take it like a woman.' And when we sting the little boys, we'd tell them to take it like a man. And Bobby Woods, he'd say, 'I can take it,' in a deep, low voice. He was the funniest boy and we used to think he was a little man, too. He's our bus driver now for Wirlomin. They were beautiful days. We used to be there, looking after the kids and every year when we used to go down to Bremer the youngest of all of us used to open the gates. We all be standing there with our buckets waiting to go into the mulberry tree. Bremer Bay has some special memories for me. They were fun days.

And Mr Dillon, he was the shopkeeper. We all had him weighed up. He was a stubborn old man. Old little bony monkey-man we used to call him. We find them cool drink bottles in the bush what other people used to throw away in the bush, not from our camp, take it to him there all this cool drink bottles. And he used to be that pleased. He'd say to other people in the shop, 'Oh, those cool drinks bottles, I gave those little Noongar kids money for them because Mr Street got them from my shop for Christmas.' Those people used to believe him. But then he found out we was finding bottles in the bush, he said, 'You can't get money off me.' That's how he never used to give us no money. So, this old man he not getting my bottle. 'We don't like you. I'm taking it to the other shop.' He said, 'I'll tell everybody in the shops around here not to give you kids anything.'

Until we let all his chooks out. We sing out, 'You not going to get any e-e-eggs.' Chookies was in them trees all over the place. He reckon, 'I'm going to kill you kids. That little fat one, she's a cheeky girl.' Let his pigs out, running with the sheep. 'You not going to give us any money so you not having any pork or chicken.' Old Dillon, he was an old wag. And after he put them all in, he forget about it. Not such a bad fella, just with this money business. They tell us to learn how to use money and him doing a thing like that, we not getting nothing, ana?

So, we'd take our bottles, but not to his shop, to another shop. We go round the back of the shop, take all them bottles and put them on the counter. 'I been saving all this cool drinks bottles.' Shop keeper'd go, 'Oh yes, sixpence, sixpence, sixpence, threepence . . .' Usually get a shilling or threepence.

We all mixed together with the other kids at Bremer. Wadjala kids. We knew them from school. They come and stay home at the camp with us. We had a ball. They only used to come there for damper. Eat all our damper on us, because after the weekend there was no bread and the old people used to make lovely damper.

We'd all race to get the biggest bream. Sea bream was the most beautiful meat. We couldn't wait. Light our own fire; cook them on the fire, the ashes. We had a little bag of salt and pepper, sprinkle it over the top. The Mission people watched what we was doing around the fire. I reckon our Mission was the best old Mission. They was pretty fair with us. The worst part, you had to do what you were told by the bigger girls or the bigger boys. Bigger boys used to get there, 'Jump in the water.' I used to hate the swimming and putting bathers on, everybody looking at my skinny legs. But I must have been a good built girl. Standing there with these little fluffy bathers they had in them days like a duck, and all that lacing at the top; I hated it.

For a while, I hated swimming in the ocean, but when the ocean used to come into the river, that was beautiful. You could see all the catfish on the bottom. The boys used to spear them, get about four or five. They eat them, but

I never used to eat them. I used to like bream. Later on, when we were there with Uncle Malcolm, I used to watch him do his fish cooking. He used to get pig face, bany, pretty pink flowers and he used to squeeze it over the fish, because that's got a lot of salt in it, you don't need salt. Stick them pigface close to the fish and then the paperbark tree, roll it up and tie it up. Well, how it used to come out! You can smell it. And the flavour is so beautiful. They were solid.

And the gum trees, we used to use that for chewing gum from the bark. You dig all them roots out and you get all them big worms. They were the sweetest worms, they was like lumps of sugar and it pops in your mouth and it was beautiful and fill you up. Fill you up. Bush tucker. And you get a sugar lump on the leaves, summertime you get them. Ants used to love them. They very sweet. I used to learn all that from the old people when I was still on the reserve. Stand and watch them what they do. Kwardiny, that's a little grass, orange thing, like a carrot. We used to chew on that. Big leaves, and you pull it up hard and it'll come out with a big piece of orange stuff. Long, it's like that sharp grass, like a knife and it's got an orangey colour. You eat it and eat it and ah, it was sweet. Only problem is if you eat too much your tongue go purple. I think that's why mine stayed purple, like a bobtail. Kids used to call me bobtail. The missionaries used to say that was poison but we ate that for a long time. Put 'em on the side of the fire and they go like a carrot; they was lovely. They even had a taste like carrot. It's funny, because a lot of Noongar women now days they don't even know nothing about that. I'm not going to tell them. I'll use it for my own.

In summer, we used to swim in the dam in the Mission grounds, a beautiful big blue dam. It was like a swimming pool. It seemed like God just made that specially for us Mission kids. They said we could go and swim in the Gnowangerup pool. Nah, dirty. Everybody swimming there. Reserve kids weren't allowed in there. That was sad. That's how the white people were them days. Very prejudiced. Terrible. Mission kids allowed in. Mission kids were allowed all over the place, even into the shops. We were one of the special ones, see, we Mission kids. And the poor Noongars they say, 'Eww, you go there? What you go there for? That's wadjalas go in that pool. Noongars not allowed there, what you going there for?' I say, 'I can.' I got new bathers and my own little towel. Run and jump in the water with the wadjalas. Wadjalas reckon, 'We going to catch you tomorrow when you come to school,' because we went to school in Gnowangerup. 'Why you want to catch me?' 'You think you wadjala, white person.' And some Noongars used to get wild with us, say, 'You with the wadjalas. You think you wadjala.' And that sort of stuck to me over the years. When we go back there now, I look at my little class. It's still standing there. I'd love to go in it one day. I can go into that school and ask for those things from the Mission school. They give things out to people now.

In our dam, it was so clean you could see right to the bottom – big djilki, maran. I don't like the maran much – too dry. We used to dive in and try to grab them. Sometimes we caught them. They got big nippers, but my toe was a bit too cunning for them. See them running towards me; I think I was a bit too fast. You see other kids got them all hanging on their feet. That's what turned me off. One look and I was off that bank. I was frightened of maran for years! Boys used to cheat sometimes with a net. That was for dinner on a Sunday. The older girls used to cook them up; you could smell it for miles. But I never liked it, and that freshwater fish, hake, or something like that, eww, I used to hate that. It had to be out from the ocean or freshwater river. That would be the best. Djilki all right. They like little prawns, nice and moist. They get up and go for walk. Years later we seen one up in Koongamia, my husband and my little boy, and this old djilki was going for a walk. We got him and put him in our bathtub, we all went to sleep, he got up and he walked out. And they don't worry about no one, eh? Talk about a wanderer.

At Easter time, we used to dye all the eggs. Chook eggs and duck eggs. Make them all colours. We had special dye, paint them up with little paintings all over and put them in the middle. I tell you, you didn't need money to make things beautiful. Ah, I can still see that Easter table. There were ribbons and everything, balloons with all paints all around it. And after we all ate them chook eggs they used to bring the chocolate Easter eggs out. Easter time we all used to go to church on Easter Sunday – be told that Jesus died for us on the cross. That stuck into my head over the years. It was the way I was brought up. United Aborigines Mission. Beautiful old church. I sketched it, old Gnowangerup Mission. All the old buildings of how I remember it at the time. In the front that big wooden boomerang sign, UNITED ABORIGINES MISSION GNOWANGERUP. It was a Baptist church. I think they were just as strict as them Catholics, but in a loveable way, because they were there by their own accord really. Never cost them nothing to come and take care of us. I am thankful now. It took years, but I look back and I'll say thank you, Lord, for helping me go through this wonderful journey.

There was sad times when I really felt like running away, but something was holding me back. That was funny, but I ended up staying there because to me it was the only home we ever had. Frightened to even walk around and run away. See all them other girls used to do it, but I did my time. They got a belting with a hose. You wouldn't be able to sit for a week.

My Dad, he felt sorry for a little boy. I told Dad, 'My buddy get hit all the time, poor fella.' So Dad said to Mr Street and them other missionaries, 'I find you belting my daughter and that little fella there, try to get away with it, I'll come and start on youse.' Other kids used to say they wish their Dads was like that. I said, 'You are, because with my Dad, everything I had, you have to have, too.' Mr Street must have said something to those others, 'He's a rough man. He'll knock anyone over.' Mr Street know – he was knocked down before by him.

We ran away twice when I was about eight or nine. I was going for the Borden reserve, but they caught us in Gnowangerup. This was a big place when you was half size and we didn't know nothing, except get going. I remember running out of the Mission down the road to Mum and Dad, but he had to bring me back, him and Mum. Told to. To me that's the saddest part. Sad times. The Mission people sent me to my dormitory. No stick or strap that time, not with Dad around.

3

Home again for a while

I WAS ALLOWED to go home with Mum and Dad, back to that same reserve in Borden and you could almost hear the echo through the trees of the old times. It was just like the sound of the breeze talking to you, telling you, well you're home now, girl. That time I just felt tears. You know that's where I was born. Mum and Dad had tears of joy. And when they spotted me, Dad, he could run! He left Mum in the dust. Come and picked me up. And Russell, he was running around by then. I was pleased to see him. I think Mum and Dad knew I was coming home, but they had no car or anything, so my old cousin said they'll bring me home to them in the horse and cart. We all thought I was home for good.

But the Welfare worked it that way where I didn't know what I was going home for. It was just to get Russell's confidence. I can't remember how long I was back with Mum and Dad on Borden Reserve, but it wasn't long, I don't think so. I look back now and I think the Native Welfare must have been conning me up for getting my little brother to come in the Mission. That's how it was. That's how they used to get us and a lot of other little kids, too. They used to say leave them there with the boys. They were hard, hard Welfares them days. Sad. And I feel sorry for all the other little kids that feel all the sadness.

Anyway, we went to Tambellup, just down the road and they came and picked us up in that police car and took us back to the Mission – the second time they picked me up. This time Russell was coming, too. He was only a little fella. He won't come to no one else, only me. And little brother he was pleased, happy, like he know he going for a ride – first time in the car. My little brother was five. I was nine. Dad was in a trip on his own.[2] Mum, well she was strong. That's how I remember Mum. I was her girl. I think it must have broke her heart. Dad, he wanted to kill everybody. 'You don't take my boy!' That was his boy, Russell. Mum taught me, 'Look after your little brother.' Dad the same. But Dad's in a world on his own at the moment and we can't seem to talk to get through to him to see what's going on.

And I asked the policeman who was driving us, 'Are we coming back to Borden?' 'You come for a ride to Gnowangerup. You'll be staying there.' That was the second time they taking me to Gnowangerup Mission. I look and

2 Documents show that Ing's father had a history of psychosis. It is conceivable that he was experiencing a psychotic episode at this time.

I can see Mum and Dad there, waving, trying to wave, that's all they can do, but they was sad. Everybody looking, aunties, uncles, all there on the side. They all cried. One hurt, everybody hurt. Then I could see my Mum and Dad walking back other way in the bush. I was crying. I was looking at my little brother. He didn't know where he was going, and then he came close to me. And I can see them waving. I knew we wasn't going to go back there to the reserve. That was hard. That's the saddest part of my life. I felt on my own. I was just a little bit bigger than when I went in first and I had the memories of what happened before. Now this happening again. And that was that – and the hurt is still there.

Mum and Dad went back to Tambellup. They went back from Tambellup to Borden the other way – through Mount Barker way. Mum had a lot of family down there in Mount Barker. Big family, too, all the Williamses. And that was really the last time we had nearly all the family together. And now we was on our own at that Mission and that's where we ended up staying.

Russell, he don't remember much; he was too small. We got very close over the years. Russell was all right. He knew all the boys at the Mission. They grew up in Borden together. There was a lot of bad things going on them days. I didn't know what it was but something was telling me that that's wrong. I could say a lot now, but I won't. I sensed something like that and I thinking, well, he my little brother, I got to watch him.

The worst part of going into the Mission is when they said you got to stop talking your language and live up to ours, white man's ways. They told me that when I went into the Mission the first time. And now they telling me again! We were all sitting down in the dining room at the Mission after we'd cleaned up and combed our hair and Mr Street the Superintendent came there and he says, 'Right, Brother Wright, another old missionary had this Mission started back then in them days.' And he said in a firm, slow voice, 'There will be no talking out loud in your language. You do what we tell you. It's time to forget that life and live our way of doing things.' At first, we thought it was funny. I wondered how can they do that? They done it. And that was sad, what they said to us. We weren't allowed to speak our language. Our mother's and father's language. Our mother's really, because Dad, he Wongi. But even if we wasn't allowed to laugh and talk in our Noongar language, we kept some of the words over the years so we knew what we was talking about. Just between the girls or the boys, and when the missionaries aren't around they'll say it and have a good laugh about it.

Some of the words that we used to talk in secret were koordany, like you'd say to a little kid. Koordany. I'm looking at you. They'd put their head down or hide behind your back. Kaanya, that means shame. Kaanya. 'You got told off, kaanya' in a teasing voice. I can't remember them now. I just went right off Noongar, but not by choice. I had to do it. And it was not long after I was put in the Mission. So, I was like a white woman in a black body. Older kids tell you, 'No, you in the Mission now. You got to do what these wadjalas tell you. We not going back to the reserve no more. You now from the Gnowangerup Mission.' And I never forgot that. You know, they drummed it in my head that much that half the time I even thought I was white!

And I still feel like it's the saddest part of my life because how we was told straight out, we not having you talking your language, you do what we tell you. If you don't do what you're told you'll get a belting for it. I had trauma when I was a little girl. I was frightened because my skin black. How come I get that colour? I used to think that. I don't know if it was frightening or I was just plain stupid.

Only thing I learnt was cooking. I learnt how to cook. I loved cooking. Never really affected me until nowadays. I'd like to find an old Golden Wattle cookbook. Old fashioned, but it's got everything in it. The Mission food was good. We had porridge. Plenty of porridge and we had plenty of fruit, apple or orange, but only if you deserved it. We used to make our own cakes and things. I got fat fairly quick. Lovely chocolate cake. One time we was cooking for a party when we were the big girls. The little kids used to do the sweeping and mopping and wash the dishes, put them away, but they was not allowed near the stoves. And Anthony's grandmother, Melva Jean Flowers, she was a bit older than me and me, Rona, Dolly and Patsy Knapp, we decided to take a visit to the dining room to see all the cakes, see how pretty they looked. Each plate we took two, ate that up. Three, four, ate all the cakes. Sat back. 'Oooh, I'm sick. I'm sick.' The little kids said, 'You done wrong. You stealing cake. You the one that put all that there. We all younger than you. You should have known better.' 'You shut up little girl, don't tell on me, I'm sick.' Then we were called to dinner. 'Eat all your dinner.' I couldn't hold it and I threw up. They knew straight away, who's the thief – Melva, Dolly and me. We all got sent to bed with nothing to eat. We didn't want nothing to eat anyway. We were full from these stupid cakes. We weren't allowed in the kitchen for a while after that. Banned all right. I was sick for a week. I learnt my lesson.

I taught myself how to cook over the years. I used to watch how everybody else do things and I do it myself. I'm up there with the best now. I say so. I don't know about anybody else. We never went hungry. There was always fresh bread. Someone makes fresh bread for us. Fresh milk. We always had fresh milk. I used to love bringing those big metal milk cans home; I didn't care how long it took to pull it over to the dining room because you'd put it in the big pot and boil that milk up. When you wake up in the morning, first thing I'd go for is the cream. And it used to be this beautiful layer of thick, fresh cream on top. That was heavenly. But you couldn't eat too much of that, it was too rich. And I used to make fresh pies and things after I learnt how to cook. Pies, pasties, sponge cake. I used to love making sponge cake. We learned how to pack all the dishes up after we finished using it, wash and clean so it's clean for the next time again. And I looked at them other kids. You know how they didn't bother. And I think most of them didn't want that kind of life. Just rough and ready. Sad.

Our beds were old-fashioned wire beds with the fold-up legs, saggy in the middle, like a cradle. We used to jump on them like trampolines and they was always collapsing on us. We put four beds together and put four mattresses on these old beds. We weren't skinny kids, little elephants. Six elephants jumping on this poor bed. We went straight through, all big fatties. And we never got caught, but all the skinny people did. We said they done it! 'Melva, Helen, Rona and Dolly, you telling lies.' And then we'd sit back and have a good laugh or yarn at night-time before we all go to sleep. We saying we done this, we done that. That's how Miss Hipwell used to catch us all the time. 'Now you just told me what you done. Stand up there, you four. You, Melva, Dolly, Helen and Patsy Knapp.' And we'd all get our smacking from that black belt inside of bike tyre before we went to sleep. We called that black snake Charlie! Weren't even allowed to talk while you're going to sleep. Too frightened to speak. Charlie might come out again.

Charlie! I hated Charlie. I put him down the toilet seat one time, because we was sick of getting this stinging off this Charlie. Poor old Miss Hipwell, she looked high and low for that black snake. We was giggling. But she got it out of us. 'Melva told me to do it.' 'She done it herself, Miss Hipwell.

Aaaah, help me, help me out!' as she getting stung by this Charlie. She never missed a beat. 'Helen, you got a problem. I'm always telling you off about something. Do you even know how to behave yourself?'

Charlie even found us when we was outside playing and didn't hear the bell. Put him in the fire, but the big boys made her another one from another tyre. That was good fun, and I think that Miss Hipwell knew that, that's why she loved us. And after she left Gnowangerup she went all the way up to Mount Margaret, work with Wongi kids up there. Most of the grown-up ones now they say, 'That old woman used to look after us in Mount Margaret Mission, old Miss Hipwell.' I say, 'She got a black snake?' 'Yeah, she made one for herself. We chase it, snaky.' I saw her once in Kalgoorlie. She was so tearful when she saw me that she couldn't speak.

And she was our old Mum down in Gnowangerup. We loved her because she taught us. She used to give us cuddles. 'Helen, I'll learn you something in life. Be sure your sins will find you out,' she used to say. And I really learnt that – I can still hear her talking about it, 'Be sure your sins will find you out.' I think that might have frightened me. I never went to jail.

It was a good Mission, not like them other missions; they belt them kids just for the fun of it, because of their skin. Them old Catholic missions, they were strict like that. Keep the Aboriginal kids out of the sun, as they going to go blacker. It's good for them. But we were family, I think that stuck us all together and kept us going. Oh no, we had everything. We had plenty of love and plenty of love to give. Run up and grab the old missionaries and say, 'Hello Uncle Tom, Auntie Beryl, Uncle Les, Auntie Olive.' They was always aunties and uncles. Sometimes I hated it. We used to run away, but get caught. I was like I was one of the Streets' family, because of Hilary, our baby sister. Even now Phillip Street, he's an old fella now, Phillip Street, he says, 'It's Ellie!' He still calls me Ellie. Well, I don't have to say too much, I just put my arm right around him. 'Fancy, those days, you was a pretty little girl,' he says.

It got so cold in winter; ice would be hanging off the long grass. We had a big open fireplace. That was the best time of the year. We'd all get into that big shed and light that mallee root fire. Little kids at crawling or kindergarten stage, put them all in a playpen and they'd be playing happy as long as you was watching them. They all had their little coats and shoes. They think I'm their auntie. So, we had a close bond with our little ones. We used to do a lot of mothercraft babies them days. Washing baby, changing nappy, listening to cries – whether the baby hungry or happy, and make sure their face was clean. They all sort of grew up in little prams and cots. We'd change their nappies, comb their hair, make them look beautiful for Sunday school, way back when.

We all had to keep our sheets clean. If they were dirty, you put them in the wash and the big boys used to boil them up and clean them for us. We only had to put them out on the line. We had plenty of rugs. Old-fashioned rugs, but they were warm. Lovely rugs. We had good clothes, sandals and socks. Dad used to buy me shoes, but if they were too small for me I'd save them for the younger girls. When littler kids than yourself used to wet their beds, I used to wash their little sheets out. I wasn't much older than they were. I must have been nine. Cold mornings, ice was that thick. Hanging them over the line, make sure they dry. Little girls would be standing, cold, cold again. It was terrible that way. Lots of little kids had chillblains because of the cold. Take them into the bathroom, put them in the bath, warm them up. The water was heated up in the copper. The big boys would do that. Girls weren't allowed near any fire. When it was bath time, the little girls went first. Scrub them down, then the big girls.

We had to bath the little kids. I hated doing that, but we had to do it. We was always shining. I must have been about nine when it was my job to help dress the little ones. Them days I didn't want to do nothing. You can't get out of it. Stay behind, hang all the clothes out. If you were caught swinging around on the floor with the kids you have to wash that floor right through. You had to do things wadjala way, white way. We don't need this. Let's run away. We ran away a couple of times. We ran to Gnowangerup. Lots of bush then. We had places to sit and hide. But the Mission people would find us. And we had to come home, get the cane, wouldn't be able to sit for a couple of days. We used to go and sit around the toilet or the big wood shed. Get all the eggs. And they were tough times sometimes, but from what I remember, they were good years of fun.

We had Jessie the cow, and a bull, Oscar his name was. Placid boy. Big, round, fat fella. Big kid. He was our pet – a prize-winner. Old Jersey bull. He was solid. They wanted him in another farm to find himself a lady. They had him in a big truck all right. We was all watching him go. He knew where the gate was and he jumped out of that truck and come running straight towards us kids. Wouldn't go courting. That's the first thing a boy will go to. Run to woman. Not this bull. Run away from the woman to come home. He'll run back with all the kids to the dining room. Big old bull standing hiding behind a tin. He stand there with his head down; he seemed to think no one was watching him. And we used to laugh our heads off. 'Oh, Oscar, you not hiding. We can see you.' Climb on top of him and he used to stand really still. We used to ride him back to his fence until they come and pick him up again. He can't get over them block ends. So, he used to go up there for a couple of weeks or a month with all the ladies and he used to come back happy. Little Oscar, he used to win prizes. It was good. And Jessie, Jessie the cow, she was so lovely. We had other cows but she was our girl. She was a stubborn old thing too. Sometimes we could ride her if she trusted you. Only the Mission kids, that's all, no one else. They knew who was the Noongars. Very fussy. They were like kids themselves.

Now, Bob Holland, he was the stubbornest sheep you ever known. He shouldn't have been a sheep! He had a human's brain. He was with this old white man but he was like Uncle Bob. We used to call him Uncle Bob, and he left that sheep with us, for the kids to play with. That sheep knew he couldn't run fast, so he picked on the smallest one out of the whole lot of us. He knows when to look for the littlest, smallest kids, he'll run after them. We be singing out, 'Look out! Bob Holland coming!' He'll stand there looking at you in a certain way, daring you. 'We're going to get hold of you, Bob Holland.' 'You try little girl and I'll knock you over.' He was thinking he was human being. Head down, he'll bump them little kids until they fall over. Goodbye bread, that's the last of it. Eat that full loaf of bread. I got knocked over once. He didn't have horns; he was one of those wethers. They used to try to get him into that field. No, he'd run as fast as his little legs can take him. Wanted to stay with us kids.

Bob Holland, he'd be standing at the door just waiting for the chance to come inside. We used to tie him up on a big string and tie a big cushion to the other end to polish the floor. Put all the little kids on this cushion or the mat and we'd say, 'Go 'way, Bob, get going.' He'd run all around that dormitory. Water flying one way, wet floor, it would be worse than when we started. I was the main actor for that. Me and Anthony's grandmother, Melva Jean Flowers. Whatever she did, I copied her, until one day we got caught and they put all the scrubbing brushes in this big bucket.

They told us, 'You can scrub that floor until they can see your face in it. And polish it.' We had our funny ways, good times there.

The big boys used to shear Bob Holland, but he never got sheared all in one go. They had to hold him down and just clipped him with scissors – a little bit here, a little bit there. Get that wool off. The old people would make little booties and little gloves for the little babies in the Mission out of that wool. Mrs Street, Miss Allen and all them old people. We all had fun then rearing them little kids up. Don't know what happened to Bob Holland; he must have died, poor old fella. Or I think someone took him for another farm.

Our Mission was like one big happy family. It was tough being taken from our family, but it was a good life. We look at other missions, how cruel they used to treat their kids. We used to get smacked, but we were never abused in other ways. That happened to a lot of the girls and boys, especially them poor little boys in other missions. That never happen to us. That was wrong from the start. I think that's what made us close and that bond that kept with us over the years growing up. We all cared for our little ones.

The boys at our Mission weren't even allowed to look at a pretty lady in a bikini them days. We go and tell the Mission people they looking at dirty pictures. Woman standing there posing in a bikini. They used to get a hiding over that. Burn the books. I think the boys learnt quicker than us. I was a dumb-dumb for years.

The different Noongar kids from the Gnowangerup reserve used to say to us, 'You mob like wadjalas.' 'No we not, we're Noongars.' 'You know more wadjala than Noongar. You think you great, just because you from the Mission,' they used to say to us. We used to get punching up with that. I learnt to fight then, because I was a bit bigger. I'd say, 'Don't do that, we're still your family.' I felt I was a black woman in a white mind. Brainwashed. I don't know if it was brainwashed, but I had to live like a white person. And years after, I remember that. True, I was glad to get out of that place. I think that's the only reason. Other than that it was a homely Mission. You my sister, my brother. For years after it always been like that. We still held that bond, even now we grandparents ourselves.

They had a hospital there at Gnowangerup Mission. That was sort of like on one side they had a little toddlers home, for little kids. On the other side, they had a big hospital there, all different, two big sets of rooms, one for operations. They had a special hospital there for Noongar ladies; about seven could fit in at a time. Mum wasn't well for Hilary in Borden, but we was in the Mission. Anyway, time went by and someone sent a message up, 'Helen, your mother is in the hospital, sick.' I said, 'She don't like hospital.' Anyway, I thinking this funny, Tow Tow [Russell] never come up. Russell Nellie never come up to see me that time. He usually come up and see me. Dad already took him down to the hospital where all these old ladies was.

I left everything and run down to see her. Mum was one of the ladies that came into the Gnowangerup Mission Hospital to have a baby! Had a look, peeped round the corner. Mummy was there, a little baby in her hands. I said, 'Who's that baby?' 'That's your baby sister. Her name is Hilary.' My baby sister was born in that hospital. I see this pretty little baby. She was so beautiful. Little pug nose. And Mummy say, 'That's your little sister. You got to look after her one day.' And Dad was sitting on the side with Russell. And that was a treasured love I'll never, ever forget. That's my little sister. And one little leg was smaller than the other. They said she was born with polio. Ah, I just put my arms right around her and cuddled her. Jumped in bed with Mummy. Mummy couldn't help laughing. I think she was overjoyed to see us. Russell piled on the other side.

That Mission hospital was the first hospital Noongars really learned to trust and get to know the missionaries. These other cheeky mob, well they get well away from them. But Noongars that were in the hospital weren't frightened of the missionaries. They trusted the missionaries. There were two old sisters in that hospital and a couple of helpers. Sister Smith, she was like the head sister with an old-fashioned thing on her head, veil, and had thermometer and everything in her pocket. The big boss there. She was a lovely old lady. She used to look after Hilary and all the other babies born in the Mission. They told Mum, 'You wouldn't be able to take her home with you, so she's got to stay with

Russell and Helen in Gnowangerup Mission.' Mum, she actually knew that. She told me, 'You're going to be mummy for her. That's your sister. You look after her.' 'She going to stay with me in the Mission?' 'Yes, you and her and Russell.' So here I wasn't much myself; I was only nine years old and I was frightened. But I knew I had a little brother to look after. Now I had my little brother and my little sister. And anyway, I'd grown a little bit. I remember them days. I think my love for them kept our love together.

Mr Street and Mummy Street, they fostered Hilary and had her as their little treasured baby and I was allowed there and Russell was allowed there, but no one else. They could see her when she was sitting outside on the veranda or somewhere. She was a beautiful little baby. And I'd carry her around, pick her up and cuddle her

Well, this Hilary, she grew on me. When she started talking and growing up and running around, chasing the kids around, she come back, 'Mummy. You like my Mum.' That broke my heart, my little sister calling me Mum. She never really knew Mum and Dad, only from visits because she was born and grew up in the Mission. Mum used to nurse her when she was a baby, but that's all. Yeah, I'd say, I'm your big Mum. 'See, I tell you,' she'd tell the other kids. She was born with polio. No one didn't know what to do about polio. We nearly lost her.

So, old Mummy Street, she took Hilary and sort of cared for her. Me and Russell used to wander in just to see

Hilary. We was one of the family there. Kids'd say, 'You not allowed to go there, that's the Superintendent's.' I say, 'I am, my sister there. C'mon Tow Tow, let's go.' Grab his hand, run up the steps. 'Mummy Street,' we sing out. And she sing out back, 'Ah, here they is, Helen and Russell.' So, we were sort of in with the Streets, like the pets of the Mission, they call us. 'Don't know what you Nellies got, but you charmed the Streets.' I tell them, 'We got our little sister.' She was a little doll.

And I used to take care of Hilary. I used to go and feed her bottles. Sometimes feed her with a teaspoon and get her and cuddle her after they change her, but she more Mr Street and Mrs Street's little girl. Like they was sole parents for her, Hilary. But me and Russell was always there. That was our little sister. She's a Nellie. She's not a Street. A fight there coming up. 'That's *my* sister!' I got mad with them a couple of times. 'You don't say nothing to me or my family. We Nellies. Our Mum and Dad was married. Mr and Mrs Nellie!'

Over the years, like nowadays, more comes up about the history of our life. Mum and Dad had fifteen other kids before me. I didn't even know that until Brother Wright said, 'You got a big family.' We were only three of fifteen other children! Got some of the names and all. I would have loved to known them. They all died, back in the forties and fifties. Some must have died when they was babies. And that really woke me up. But times then was real hard. Because back then they never had medicines. Old Noongars, they was just coming out of bush country into reality. Noongars was getting strange sicknesses they never had before. There was no doctors. All they had was herbs and honey, wild honey, lemon. Them days they was all frightened of the doctors, white doctors. They thought they was different people – out of this world. I consider myself very lucky. I had old people explained it to me, who I am. I think I must have been one of the lucky ones, the last of the old generation.

We weren't allowed to go out any time, but Mum and Dad used to come up to the Gnowangerup Mission. The Mission was three miles out of Gnowangerup town, just on the hill. You can see the town from the Mission. That's where we was. And Mum and Dad used to come from Borden on the old diesel train to see us at the Mission. They'd come once a month or maybe twice a month. It was good that way. I still had Mummy and Daddy. My Mum was my heart. She was really caring. And there was a lot of families. Anyone who had a family, their mothers and fathers used to come up and see them, come up and see all their children from time to time. They was allowed to do that. And that was the best.

When they saw our Mum and Dad, everybody there before me. But we had to share, me and my brother, we shared with all them other kids our Mum and Dad's love. What they buy me and Russell, they saved it for last. They give all the other kids some first. You know, lollies and cool drinks and biscuits for the kids, make sure they all had a little bit each. And then they'd go back and give ours. They were very caring old people, them two. But he was a cunning old man, my Dad; he used to hold ours in a separate bag. I used to like them liquorices, Choo-Choo bars; all your mouth is black. Used to cost threeepence in the Mission for a little one.

I used to hate them ribbons they put on your hair at the Mission. I reckon they were ugly looking things back then. Till I cut my hair short. Got into trouble for that, but it turned out okay. It was like mushroom haircut before. When I cut it, it was fashion, in the 60s, so I didn't mind that. I was in the fashion before the other girls. And they pulled a little piece of hair trying to put a ribbon on. They said, 'No, just leave her. She looks okay as she is.' Everybody else wanted to get their hair cut like that. And nobody wearing ribbons anymore, so we had to wear these silly little straw hats, them little pretty ones with the ribbons in the back. Oh, I hated that.

Old Miss Hipwell was like a domestic science lady. She had a hump back. She taught us from a young age how to cook scones and pikelets and apple pie. I used to love making apple pie. She was an angel, but not all the time. Sometimes she was like an old witch. But now I look back, she was our angel, a God-sent angel. If we was naughty, we would deserve to get the strap. Hit with the hose, switchy stick, cane, or Charlie. 'Look out, snake coming.' Sit down. We wasn't even allowed to talk. Someone in trouble, I sit there, like an angel. 'Oh, Helen I'm very pleased with you with your hands crossed.' Same time I'm kicking Dolly or Rona. They tried to push me away. 'Miss Hipwell, Helen kicking me here.' 'No she's not, she's got her arms folded and looking up to the ceiling.' They used to call me a con woman. Yeah, had all that.

I was one of the naughty ones when I went into the Mission the second time. I didn't want to do what everyone else had to do. Let's go. Me and my cousin, Melva Jean, we was always into trouble. We used to walk halfway to Borden before that one-way truck from the Mission, the United Aboriginals Mission, would come and realise we were heading home to Borden, to our home, our home town. We got a hiding over that! And that was that. They said, 'You come back. You're going to do what you are told. You can wipe your way of life out. You won't be going back there no more. You learn white man's laws.' Ah, I hated it. Had to learn their way of living. You could hear the kids shouting until the bell rings for tea. Or someone wants to talk to somebody, they usually ring the bell and we all have to run and line up and then they'd call the kid they wanted to talk to. Often it was me – always in trouble.

A lot of people say they were treated bad. It wasn't like that in our Mission. If you was naughty you'd get a good hiding or you'll stay behind, scrub floors. They don't let you near the kitchen unless you was working there. For punishment, that kitchen was out of bounds, especially for me. I go looking for chocolate cake or lollies. 'No, Helen's not allowed in the kitchen. We won't have nothing left for nobody else.'

We were good girls, all right. We made toffee apples. Burnt all the sugar, vanilla and all that to make the toffee. Painted the colours. The apples come out lovely and red and shiny. Put them down there on the side. 'Hmmm, I wonder how it'll taste.' True, me and Melva. You sitting down and Miss Hipwell would say, 'Okay Dolly, put your hands on your head and Helen, you the main actor, Helen. Put your hands on your head. Melva and Louise, put your hands on your head. Whoever took those toffee apples will be found out.' We all looking at each other, 'Put your hands on your head.' You couldn't laugh. She'd be just up there sitting in the big dormitory lesson room writing a letter or something.

The dormitory had a big long passageway and about one, two, three, four places where all the beds was and the passageway with a big long mat. And then you got a bathroom on the side and this big lesson room and a kitchen where we can learn to cook.

Well, Miss Hipwell, she had us in that lesson room. We had to sit on the floor. 'Now, which one of you girls, honestly tell me who took them toffee apples. You'll know because you'll get a tummy ache anyway while you're sitting down there.' We all be looking at each other, smiling, giggling, pulling faces, want to talk. 'No talking!' she'd say. She'd know what's going on. It's her way of getting the truth out of us. 'I'll know out of all you seven girls who's the thief, but I'll leave that up to the Lord Jesus. That will be the first one with the feather on their nose.' We're sitting there like little angels, me and Melva, thinking hard about not touching our noses. Drop our hands. 'Put your hands back. You can stay a bit longer.' She never used to miss a beat. She knew our every move. We whisper to each other, 'You old witch. Let's run away.' Straight away she say, 'No one is going to run anywhere.' She got ears! For an old lady she got ears like a bat.

And we sitting there with our hands on our heads and our noses start twitching itchy. Try to ignore it, but that itch is getting worse, like someone in my nose playing with it. And this thing was starting to work, whatever it was, magic spell or something. And when she said, 'Be sure your sins will find you out,' we was looking straight at her, screwing our nose up, not with snot, it's just the Lord tickling our nose. Another girl, she was trying to put her tongue up her nose to scratch it, but her tongue wasn't long enough. My nose twitching and wriggling and my tummy aching. Then noses start running. Couldn't wipe our nose without getting a smack on your hand. And this is how she found out who was eating all the toffee apples. Guilty twitch. That is how we got our sins caught out. She must be killing herself laughing. 'Melva and Helen, you are very bad. You can stay behind. All the rest of you can go. Your noses are clean.' 'How did you know, Miss Hipwell?' 'Don't you worry. Satan got his ways.' And that Charlie coming out around that corner. I said, 'Noooo,' standing with one leg pulled up, covered with hands so there is not so much for Charlie to sting. 'I'm sorry, I'm sorry. Don't hit me Miss Hipwell.' We had to sit there and say, 'Sorry, Lord Jesus,' tell Him our troubles. Then, 'Get up and have a shower and behave yourselves.' It wasn't funny at the time, but look back on them years and we sit down now laughing. My main punishment was I was sick for a full week, so I couldn't do much. It was a good excuse. Those other girls all was tossing and turning. 'We not following you any more, Helen.' 'Not me,' I say. 'You come in yourself.'

Miss Hipwell, she was the most treasured old woman. Very wise and very clever. Very strict old lady; she was strictly on the bible, but a good old teacher. She must have thought we were devils. We hated her at the time, dear Lord forgive me. 'Be sure your sins will find you out.' I can still hear her talking.

There was another old angel, Auntie Bonnie Knapp, worked in the Mission. Albert's mother. Me and him and Russell, we was very close. We used to help her when she made curtains. We were allowed to go for walks in the hills around the Mission with her every winter. Get all beautiful big, pink mushrooms and that was our winter treat. Used to walk for miles looking for tiny, long little red berry and koomak, koorep, cummock, same little tiny green sweet berry that hangs from the vines of trees down south, mal, Bobtails love them. They go pink and then red when they ripe. They fall when they ripe, lovely and sweet. And there's a lovely soft pink flower; they got beautiful fruit on them and they're lovely and sweet. You can mix them in sugar and eat them like lolly. That was heavenly. Cook them up on the side of the fire and roll them all in sugar. That was like a lolly itself. Ground berry, beautiful red flower. It's there all the time, but in midsummer it'll be out, lovely, like a carpet. Beautiful that was. Orange thing like a carrot, Kwardiny. Bush medicine. We used to chew on that. And the sugar potatoes; see a rainbow flower and dig underneath and it was so sweet and you'd never go thirsty. And get the kwandangs to make jam. In midsummer it'll be beautiful and sweet.

Tambellup was the first place I attended school after I first went into the Mission and come out with Mum and Dad that time. Never had long there before they come and picked us up and took Russell and me to the Mission. Then I used to go to the school in Gnowangerup. I think I only went up to grade six in the Gnowangerup Junior High School. I loved sport. I was a champion runner. Basketball! I used to trip all the other kids over. Always getting into trouble for that. Miss Gelmi, my teacher at Gnowangerup Junior High kept threatening and telling me if I don't behave myself and stop fighting with one of the boys I won't be going home on the bus. I said I don't mind. I can walk home. I won't go home, I'll go to the reserve. She whacked me, so I got in and whacked her back. (She whacked me first.) I grabbed the teacher and give it to her with the cane what she whacked me with. I was a big girl them days and I thinking she not going to come to me like that. That was it. The game was on. They said okay we give you until the end of the week and you don't come back to school here.

I got thrown out of the school. I was sad for that. I say I was chucked out because I knew too much. Miss Gelmi was a beautiful teacher. I felt that terrible after. She was very good to me. She'd be an old lady now. I never went back to school. I don't mind. I was working around the Mission. You know, laughing at the kids all going to school, 'Ta-ta.' 'Ooh, we going to tell on you. You can't laugh at us.' 'I don't have to go to school. I've finished school.' Even boys at school, even man, now, in Gnowangerup say, 'Helen, you never change. You used to belt us all the time when you was a little girl. We used to run away from you.' I'd tell them, 'You listen to my brother or you get a hiding.'

A lot of the girls used to leave the Mission, come back to the Mission, all pregnant, waiting for babies. I saw a lot of little kids born at the Mission hospital. Young girls. Frightened me! I'm not going to be like that. They was taught what boys meant to do and what girls meant to do – and don't do it. I refused to do anything. The first real kiss in my life was when I was 22 or 23. Scared of boys. You come close to me and you'll get this fist. I used to frighten them away.

4

Tragedy strikes

RUSSELL AND ME and all the little kids would look forward to my Mum and my Dad coming to the Mission. They come and seen us at the Mission for the last time. Fed all the kids first, then they give me and my brother some. See the big ute coming around the corner. I had a funny feeling. I couldn't describe it. My cousin come and tell me, 'I'm going to Narrogin with my Auntie and Uncle, your Mum and Dad. They coming for a ride with us to old Uncle's funeral.' I said why Narrogin? Can't they have it here? Mum said, 'We going with them for a ride.' Put them on that ute. My cousin was driving and away around the corner. And I thinking, oh they'll come and see us again soon. Then that horrible thing happen. That was the last time I seen them alive.

I think I must have sensed something there. Sensing real deep down. Can't find the words, but this happening to me. This day, it wasn't the same. I was working with all these little baby kids, little kindergarten kids, helping the lady down there, look after them, wiping their faces and doing their toys. But I kept on feeling that something wasn't right that day. I was real unsettled like. Now I look back and I'll say I knew that something was happening.

At the Mission, in every part of the dormitory there was about one, two, three, four, five, six beds. My bed was next to the window in the middle and the big window there, you could see for miles. That night we was all sitting there talking and scratching pictures, laughing about how stupid we was, doing this and doing that. I was sitting on that bed. Other girls was there, all playing. And this night no wind was about but the curtain flew up in the air. And all of a sudden my bed just come up into the air and a little bit away from the wall. Just went out and it must have been a little minute and it come back and down, slowly. I thinking, hey look there, Mummy, Mummy. No wind at all. And when the girls said look at the window and I look, my mother was there. Spirit. Her spirit was right there. I couldn't say nothing. Just paralysed me. She come to me and said goodbye. But being in my early teens, I never realised that. But she come to me when she died. And I can see her even now, standing there, smiling. Wanted to touch me. I couldn't do nothing. Cold. It was there and next minute it's gone.

When I sort of come to, the girls was still looking there, all started talking and then a minute later looked, nothing, warm again. There must have been about four girls in the room with us. They was that scared and they took off down the hall. They run screaming, but I was like I was stuck there, just looking at the window. I couldn't move. I was frightened, but I was speechless. Mission people, they come running when they hear all this screaming. 'What's the matter? What's the matter you kids? What's frightening you kids?' 'No, Helen's bed come up in the air out of nowhere.' And they all come peeping round the corner, 'You all right?' 'Yeah.' I got up and walked out after and they reckon they seen that. 'That was your Mum, eh?' they say to me. 'Yeah, that was my Mum.'

Something happen. It was my Mum. She was killed. Come to say goodbye. Telling me she won't be around. You know I'll always be with you. You got my heart. Her spirit come back to me when she got killed telling me she can't stay with me. I believe that. That's my Mum. I can still see her. Girls wouldn't come back, but I laid on my bed, had the best sleep.

And a day after they was already gone, me and Russell were told, 'You wanted at the office.' I was about thirteen. Russell was a little fellow about ten. I said, 'What for?' 'Dunno. You must be going home to your Mum and Dad, you and Tow Tow. Police want to see you.' But I already knew something was wrong. This lovely sunny day and I look, yeah, two policemans standing there at the office, Sergeant Bayswater, and another policeman. Mr Street, Auntie Bonnie looking at us. Police said, 'Hello Helen, how you going in school?' 'Good.' I didn't tell him I been chucked out of school. 'And Russell?' I thinking I'm going home. I must have hurt poor old Mr Street. Anyway, he put his hand around me and I thinking this funny, this funny. Something must have happened, but I already knew something happened. Mr Street he says, 'You been a good girl, Helen? You look after your little brother?' 'Yes, Uncle Tom.' They already told all the other kids and the missionary and they weren't allowed to say nothing to me or Russell. That's all I knew. And then the policeman told us that Mum got killed in a car accident and Dad, he's in Narrogin Hospital. 'Your Mum was killed instantly. Came out the streets in Narrogin yesterday afternoon. Noongars was on the back of a ute going to your Uncle's funeral in Narrogin. Your Mum and Dad was one of the people there.' Russell was a little fellow but I was old enough to understand what was death. When someone die, well they going away and leaving us. You won't see them no more.

It's just like my world just stood still. I looked at my little brother. 'Your Mum went to heaven but your Dad is still in hospital.' And that time my nephew, Ronnie Williams, he just turned his life to be with the Lord, Jesus. And Ronnie went straight away to the hospital in Narrogin because that was his grandparents, see. And he went straight there and he was the only one close to me and Russell, other than Albert. He said, 'I'll go with Mr Scott.' When they went there, Dad asked him, 'My boy, go get me a cup of tea. Where Mummy?' 'Oh, she's here,' he said. But she weren't there. Well, she was there, but she was dead. Ronnie telling me after, Dad, he drank that cup of tea and then he died. Mummy must have said, 'Well, I'm not going without you. You might as well come.' Powerful. And I had that feeling I think he could have done that at that instant. Ronnie told me the same thing. All he wanted to find out where Nan was. Ronnie told me years after, 'I was there with Pop and he told me, "I know Mum's here. She's by my side." He had that last cup of tea, just held my hand and went to sleep. They together,' he said. And Mummy would have said, 'I'm going to tell Ing.' I'm sure Mummy would have said that. One day she already sleep.

My Mum and my Dad, dead. And I didn't know what to do. My world just stopped.

So life wasn't the same, because we used to see Mum and Dad every weekend, second weekend, really. They used to buy all the children in the Mission biscuits and lollies. Me and Russell, we were the last two to get things off Mum and Dad. And all the children in the Mission used to love those two old people. When I looked, I wasn't the only one to have a broken heart. All the kids that was there, they didn't know what to say to me. I couldn't understand it, but one of the big girls said, 'Your Mum and Dad are all right. They're going to see us all the time because they in heaven.' And I think that's how I got through life. But I knew they left me with my little brother and my little sister. By this time my little baby sister, Hilary, started crawling around. She learned to walk but had to wear calipers.

The Mission people took Russell and me to Mum and Dad's funerals. They was buried together one day apart in the Gnowangerup cemetery. One on top of the other in the grave. I know exactly where they are buried. One day I want to get a headstone or a plaque for them. Put their name on it. I was a bit young them days, but I remember where they buried them, right in front. And I'm going to get one for my son and my little sister. Unknown to anyone I had about fifteen other sisters and brothers. The two girls I see and the one boy name there. The other ones are in the old cemetery place on the other side of the fence.

And Ronnie, he said he couldn't cry, because he knew the Lord Jesus then and knew the Lord was with us. But he sort of got close to me and Russell and Albert. He was our nephew even though he was older than us. He was boss. I remember him first coming to the Mission, Ronnie. Little baggy short pants on, barefoot, shanghai over his shoulder what he kill birds with. And he said – sing really – 'Hello all the kids. I come to see my Auntie and Uncle.' 'Who your Auntie and Uncle here?' 'Auntie Ing and Uncle Tow Tow. That's my Auntie and that's my Uncle.' Before he ever become a Christian he used to come up to the Mission and see us all the time, give us a shilling or two bob. Always save that prize for me and Russell. 'That's my little Auntie and little Uncle.' He had the funniest voice. I say to the other kids, 'Shut up, that's my nephew'. They laugh, 'Look at the size of him to you. You little Auntie?'

Mum must have been 54 when she was killed. Dad, he was in his 60s. Quite a young fellow. And she was a lovely person. I have the papers about Mum and Dad's accident. It makes me cry. I still have my tears every time I read it. So, I hardly read it.

We had Uncle Tom and Mummy Street after we lost our parents and that's how we all got by. Knowing we had someone there to be looking after us, I think that's what got me through the worst part of my life, trying to get over that Mum and Dad going and settle myself down to . . . nothing, but my little brother and sister. That was the hardest thing I had to do, because every time I look at them I see Mum and Dad. I stuck to them. Still, you look up and see if you can see them. No one comes.

That was the worst test in life, was when I realised I have to be there for my little brother and sister. That's how life made me strong. I had to be. Even when Russell started growing up he used to call me Mum. 'I'm your sister.' 'Nup, you Mum.' And Hilary, my little sister, used to call me Mum. Hilary used to say to me, 'I know where Mum and Dad went. They went to heaven. They must have been sick of us.' I tell her, 'Don't talk like that. That was an accident. That's our Mum and Dad.' You feel like crying and yet you got to try to explain this to this little sister. Russell used to chase her around when she make me sad like that. Make her run away. He come back, 'You right now?' he say to me. And I used to sit down and have a good old cry on my own.

Russell, he was my inspiration in life. He's always been in the back of my mind, doesn't matter what I do or say. We're very close.

And Auntie Bonnie Knapp, dear old angel, used to say to cousin Albert, 'Well, that's your little brother and sister there. They got no Mum and Dad. You bigger than them. It's your place to look after them.' I think that saved us, too, because Auntie Bonnie was a powerful old lady. She was a really good Christian lady. I even used to call her Mum. Then she sort of grew old; age sort of caught up with her and they took her back to Gnowangerup to rest. She was my power, too. Tell me things I shouldn't do and what I should do, explain everything to me. And I used to listen to Auntie Bonnie. That's one of the best things I ever done.

And Albert, he's still a big, big brother for us. We always looked up to Albert. Even now we look up to him. We always had Albert on our side. He was our big brother. He had plenty of his own family, all the Knapps and the Haywards and that. No, he'd come to us, 'I'm just going to have a look and check on my little sister and brother.' Other mob didn't like it much. 'He's *our* brother.' Even now, he looks after us and he don't like doing things unless I'm there. 'Ing, you coming? Come on, you come with us.' I'll say, 'I'm right behind you, brotherrrr.'

And I think that having to look out for Russell and Hilary made me feel strong within myself. I keep telling them that. I can get by. But without Mum and Dad I used to look around and the kids in the Mission were pleased to see their Mum and Dad, but they never used to go near them. They were frightened. I dunno if it's the upbringing or what. Frightened to even say that's my Mum and Dad. I think it was because a lot of little ones was in there from when they were babies and they didn't know who their Mum and Dad are. When my Mum and Dad was alive, all the kids used to run and grab them. They were beautiful old people. That's the main history of my Mum and Dad. They were always there for us. Doesn't matter where we were.

Took me years to get over Mummy's death. She was close to me. She used to call me her heart. Russell was Daddy's boy. And now every time we go past that same spot where they got killed in Narrogin, going down home, that big white bird comes right over top of us, me and my brother Russell. Both of us see it every time. Never miss. Sort of like a bit smaller than a Wedgetail Eagle. I say, 'Don't feel frightened, don't be frightened. That's only Mum.' Well, she's watching us, guiding us through. That's Mummy guiding us home, a guardian angel, they say. That's your guardian angel. That's my Mum. Russell he drive along. Stop the car, say goodbye. See you next time. Then we go home. No worries. So, she's still with us.

Every time my brother comes to see me, she let me know, '*Your brother be here tonight.*' I get a feeling. She do things like drop a fork on the floor or move a cup or something. Bang on the wall. So, she's still with us.

Mum was the youngest. She must have been a picture, Mum. All my old aunties they'll say I got my mother's own face. 'She's not dead. She's in you.' Old aunties used to tell me a lot about Mum. Told me she was smart. She never mess around for no one. Old Pooya, Dad, had to run through the bush to catch her up. She was pretty, her hair was reddish and long. She must have been a charmer. And I can see why I was her heart. I know she's always in my heart. Sometimes she lets me know, too. 'You're my girl.'

5

The Mission closes

OUR MISSION WAS more like a family Mission – a good Mission. People in other missions must have had a hard time compared to us. Ours was more like learning, teaching us. Taught us what was right from wrong. Taught us to behave ourselves because we not on the reserve anymore and all that sort of thing. Oh, we got into trouble if you done anything wrong. We used to know that. We used to look at the town three miles down the road. That's too far, we can't run. Run through the bush night-time. Never used to worry about a thing. That was the best part of it. I was always in that, just for the fun of it. Right till I turned sixteen year old. Always get caught, but that just new adventure.

We been brought up as a family, one family. That was the Woodses, Williamses, Nellies, Roberts and Flowers. We were taught that right from when we first went in. If we got into trouble we got a hiding for it or scrub the floors. I was always scrubbing floors. I never knew if I had knees or what in the end. But they were good. They punished us, but let us go in the end. They had no choice.

I always thought that Gnowangerup Mission was going to be my home till I get old, that no one will ever go anywhere. Then one day in 1962 that bell rang in the old dining room. Ding ding ding ding ding. A little after lunch, we all had to go and sit in the dining room. Mr Scott and Mrs Scott was in charge then. Mr Devenish, Mr Power, Mrs Power, all their kids. We sort of grew up with them. They was all one of us. I remember walking into that dining room. Everybody all laughing and happy as anything, until Mr Scott said, 'I want all of you to hold hands.' So we sort of shuffled around in a big circle. That's when I knew something was happening. 'You know, all you children. I come to tell you this. We can't get any funding to keep our Mission going.' And everything went quiet. We didn't know what to say, because that was our home, only home we ever knew in our life growing up. 'What's going to happen to us? Where we all going Mr Scott?' 'Well, we sending some of you to Roelands Mission near Bunbury, and Katanning, Marribank Mission. Some will be going working, if you want to. Family groups will be sent to Marribank.' Didn't even know where Marribank was. Marribank was called Carrolup. Old Carrolup is next to Katanning. 'If you all want to stick together that's where you'll be going, to Carrolup. Helen is finished. She can stay here until the Mission is completely finished and then she'll have to get a job.'

That was really upsetting for all of us. Everybody just stood and looked and then we just put our arms around each other and had a good cry. Even the missionaries all had tears. That's when I started growing up, I think, growing up on my own. I knew I'm going to be on my own and I have to live up to it. My little brother and sister! I got a brother and sister! They need me more than anything else now. I knew I had to get out and go to work. But I didn't want to leave the only home I had in my life. I was a little bit bigger then. I knew a little bit about saying goodbye and saying sorry for things. I felt terrible. This was my home. I always thought that Gnowangerup Mission would go on for us, even like when we leaving the Mission, we got a home to come home to. Wasn't meant to be. Broke my heart. I was finished school and I was looking at all these little kids, all standing up and holding hands with these other little fellows around this big table. Mr Scott praying for us. There aren't going to be no more Mission here now. Then the tears really started. I will never forget that, never.

When we back to our dormitories, very quiet children. Never hardly said anything. 'We going away?' 'Must be.' 'Where you going? You coming with us?' 'No, don't think so.' How could they do this to us? We was still under Welfare, see. Most of the bigger kids, that was the only home they had, too, after their Mum and Dad left them. It was frightening.

The Mission closing! It would have been all right if they'd have said, you could stay at the Mission until you sort your own lives out, but we all had to move. Where I going to go? How am I going to survive?

About a month after we was told the Mission was closing, Russell and Hilary were sent to Marribank. Carrolup, old Carrolup, in Katanning. That's just down the road from Gnowangerup about 25 miles. I felt terrible. It still hurts now. Now we going to be distance apart. But there's nothing I could do. I was still a State Ward. I don't think Hilary was because she was born in the Mission. I saw them when I could afford to, on the weekends and that. Mr Scott usually come and pick me up and drop me home, back in Gnowangerup or I'd get a ride with my nephew or my cousins.

So I had no little sister and brother to look after and I was in care of Miss Wade and then after she told me, 'You have to go and stay at cousin Rita's. She could be your boss.' 'What?' Strange, me going back on that Gnowangerup reserve. Years ago I been there for just a little while and that's when life sort of come to me all in a rush. I got nothing. No Mum and Dad. How am I going to face my family? What do I have to say to them? I don't know their ways. Do it somehow. Frightening. I was frightened to even go back on the old reserve and even look at my family – Borden, Gnowangerup, Albany.

Broke all our hearts when the Mission closed down. It was 1962. I was going on for sixteen and that was another big, sad time in my life – another big heartache. We didn't know how to face life. They took us from home and brought us this far, telling us how to live that far. But we don't know where to go, what to do. It was like I was stuck. I was old enough to understand a little bit about life. How I been brought up was that I always thought that no one will ever leave the Mission, that no one will ever go anywhere but it wasn't meant to be.

I'm glad I went through it, you know and I look back over the years at these other children from Roelands and Marribank. They had a hard life. And I couldn't understand why because most of them say the Mission people will either give you a hiding or the girls get and have children by the missionary boys and that. I think the boys learnt quicker than us. I was a dumb-dumb for years. Forget about the rough times and the sad times. There were plenty of sad times. But Gnowangerup Mission was strong. Not only made us strong, but we learnt how to live white man way. That part will never go away.

I been blessed somewhere along the line. I think Mum was with me. And even though I was frightened when I was finished in the Mission, old people at the Gnowangerup reserve used to tell me, 'You come back to us. This is your home, with us. No Mission no more.' I had wonderful old aunties who knew what we was, what Russell was going through. But they said, 'He's too young yet. When he's a bit bigger, he'll come looking for you. But you got to learn to live Noongar way now because there's no more Mission.' I think that was the most frightening thing in my teenage life. Now I'm going to get on the reserve. I'm not going to like living on a reserve. These Noongars don't want me. But I was wrong, because my Uncle Malcolm, my mother's brother was always there for me, pushing me to do something.

I told my old Uncle out of the blue, 'Remember me, Uncle Malcolm?' And I said to his wife, 'You my old Auntie?' He come and put his arm around me. 'You're my sister's daughter. You're not on your own.' That's what he said to me. 'By the time I finished with you, you'll know everything. I love you, you my girl,' he says. 'You my Ingawoo.' It's like yesterday he was saying that. I never forget that and I think that's what made me strong over the years. He said, 'Rita, look after her. Just remember, she not on her own, that's my girl, my sister's child.' 'Thank you, Uncle Malcolm.' 'No, I'm here for you.' So, I stuck my head up in the air and walked with him. Things he told me, you can dig that sand and it lets you know, every little grain, what happened in the old days. Even now, I can see him close.

6

Learning to be Noongar again

WHEN I FIRST come out of the Mission, I went to the Gnowangerup Aboriginal Reserve. That was terrifying. It's a terrible feeling going back into a Noongar community when you've been forbidden to be Noongar. I was frightened. I didn't want to go there. When I first went there when the Mission closed my gang used to say to me, 'You're a wadjala in black woman's skin.' It's true; I thought I was wadjala – white lady. But I was frightened because my skin black. How come I get that colour? I used to think that. I don't know if it was frightening or I was just plain stupid. They reckon, 'Yeah, you Noongar, but you white woman.' And I never used to understand what this was all for. It wasn't my fault. We weren't allowed to be Noongar at the Mission because these whitefellas was teaching us their ways and there was nothing else to do except learn it. We had to do it. I wouldn't want to go through that again.

My family used to call me wadjala woman. 'You been

with wadjalas too long.' No, I haven't. This my country just as much as yours. They reckon, 'We Noongars, we been brought up on the reserve, but you haven't. You, you know nothing about reserve life.' They got the STOP RIGHT THERE sign. I say, 'I know, the reserve not my place. I'm a Mission girl and I'm proud I had my training. I can get to places where you can't.' 'Eww, who you think you is?' I say, 'You want to say wadjala, say wadjala. I'm simply Ing.' They go, 'Don't talk to that wadjala woman,' or 'You not like any other Noongar, but you've got a black body.' I used to hate people when they say that. 'You come to our life. You a Noongar. This is your country. You got to live with us. Start from the start.' My aunties used to say to them girls that tease me, 'You girls, you'll never come up to Ing. Ing is a wadjala girl, even though she is dark, you'll never come up to her.' And I reckon that was sad, really sad. That was the hardest time of my life. The hurt, listening to people. And I thinking well I'm big enough, why should I listen to everybody?

Going through teenage life, I was stubborn. One day I said to myself I had this attitude but I got no one. I needed to find out who I am. Who my family? I was still working myself out. Mission life was still there and it is there forever that I was a Mission girl. And I thinking I have to be changing it. No one else going to change me. I'd have to change myself. A lot of it was that I was shy, frightened to talk out. Sister Audrey, Hazel's sister, she was my rock. She used to say to me, 'You got a tongue. Talk up, girl, talk up.' So I changed to a rowdy person and I think everybody was sick of me by then. Glad to get rid of me. They couldn't tell me nothing. I was off. Really argumentative with everybody. It was unfair. I was sort of a young girl and a teenager and I had to grow up by myself, really. I had aunties and uncles who tell me who I am. 'You Nellie.' I think I be thankful for that.

They had their own way of life. I used to watch them all get drunk. They say, 'You going to have a smoke with us, Ing?' 'No. What's that?' Never used to smoke, never used to drink till I got into my twenties. But my brother, Gerald, he my first cousin because his mother and my mother was two sisters. He was working out on the farm and he had three daughters. One day I'm following my nieces down to the big old dam where their father used to work. 'Come with us Auntie Ing, come with us Auntie Ing.' We dancing on top of this big dam at this farm, dancing in petticoats and bras, just being stupid teenagers. Little kids was with us. My little niece, she was only six. 'Oh you want a cool drink, Auntie?' 'What cool drink? No one got cool drink here.' 'Here Auntie, have a drink of this cool drink,' she said. 'Have a good drink.' Big bottle of Emu Export. Well, I had a good drink of this cool drink because I was thirsty. 'Here, have that one too. It's good for you!' Beer! One bottle of Emu Export got me paralytic drunk and they gave me another one! Two big bottles of Emu Export. Couldn't finish it. One bottle I could see two people; two bottles I could see three people! That was the first time I ever tasted beer in my mouth. My little niece!

She's supposed to be at school. I just lay back, let it roll. Never used to smoke, either. Smoke! Never smoked until I was in the forties mainly, that's when all the worries of the world started settling on my shoulder and I just didn't know where to go. I sort of one at a time, one at a time. Oh well, you live and learn. That's the time I really started. First time I got choked. Spun me right out. Never again. And that was old Rothmans. The worst smoke. That was the horriblist smoke. Never ever take that again.

But that day with the beer! My brother come back. He could have killed them two little girls. 'She can't drink, she's a Mission girl!' Yeah, always attitudes like that. They'll throw that weight at their kids you know. 'We know that's your Auntie, but she's a Mission girl. She don't drink. She don't smoke, so don't even introduce her to that. I'll pull my belt off to you and give you a good hiding.' 'Sorry Dad,' and she run back, crying. 'You get us in trouble all the time,' they say. They blame me!

My sister Molly told me afterward, she reckon that I couldn't talk. She told Theresa, my niece, 'Theresa, you know you got your Auntie drunk, you should be the one to get a hiding; you should be the one to get told off. A shame on you. She never drink anything like that, she come from the Mission, wadjala girl.' 'No,' my niece said, 'She not wadjala, she like me, pretty colour.' Theresa, she was beautiful. Beautiful little niece. And that was funny days. And my old brother come, he call my name. 'You come along with us. I'm taking you out bush with us.' So I used to go out with them. All them brothers they was cheering. They used to love me. And they all took me out, teach me Noongar ways.

Once, their wives, about five of them all sitting around the table. I ask, 'What all you fellas doing?' They reckon, 'You be doing tea tonight.' 'Why? I never done this bush tucker in my life.' And they said, 'You make a damper and a stew.' Well, the stew was like the Black Sea – it smelt like salt. The damper was like the Stirling Ranges, all burnt. Well, when the brothers come back they said, 'Who done this awful cooking?' One brother, he said, 'I'm putting it on my tent. I can see the Stirling Ranges right here with this damper.' 'Ing done it!' Well, I felt sorry for them women. They got the biggest hiding. 'She don't know nothing about Noongar ways. Why let a silly girl like that do things?' And I felt shamed.

Years later when I was living in Perth I was in a competition at Koongamia Primary School when my son, Anthony, was at school. Them school people tell the Noongar mothers, 'Come and show us your skills.' We had a damper making and a big pot of stew and ah, I was lucky that day. It was supposed to be for kangaroo and emu, little bit of emu, but I had beefsteak in it. Tell everybody this was kangaroo and emu. No herbs or anything in it. That was the loveliest feed I think them poor little kids had. I made the best dampers. I can still see them all lining up for it. They said, 'Anthony, every time your mother do something she always wins. We don't think she should come here anymore.'

But back on the reserve my brothers said, 'Come along little sister, come along with us.' So, they took me to the shop in Borden. I didn't know nothing about money. I didn't know what money was. I didn't worry about it. Everything was bought for me. The first time I had a roll of money in my hand my old cousin left me; I didn't know what to do with it. I reckon these are pretty paper notes. Ten pounds. I looked, aah, look here, another ten pounds on top of that. This must be the money. I put them all in my pocket. My brothers, about six of them, all shearers. And I had my money's worth at that Gnowangerup shop.

Uncle Malcolm, when I got back said, 'What they give you at that shop?' I said I got Rice Cream, a tin of Rice Cream and peaches. They said, 'What?' Yeah, well I never used to smoke, never used to drink, just eating the sweet stuff. I had Christmas on that Rice Cream and peaches, big dash of cream on top. 'Rice Cream? No wonder you fat!' I said, 'I'm used to this, we used to have all of this in the Mission.' He said, 'But this isn't the Mission, this is the reserve.' I give some to all the little kids; make sure they have some too. I always share. He said, 'You know what? You're just like your Mum.'

Even though I didn't know about money, shopkeepers, they had to be honest. My brothers was there. You don't say nothing to our family. But they all sort of went to school together. See, a bit older than me, but the shop boss, he knew the family's history see. And another time they teach me how to do this wool, pull all the whole wool off the thing and chuck it on the table. Go right around. That was good because I learnt that wool baling. Got good money for that. It was hard work. Stunk to high heavens, some of it. They taught me how to get on with my game and to work it out.

And they had an old horse and cart. I remember riding on that old horse and cart. My cousin, he was coming back and he was telling Dad, Uncle Malcolm, that he was coming home, on the shortcut through West Burridges in Gnowangerup, going through to Tambellup. He was coming back to Gnowangerup Reserve. And where this place was my uncle shot his stepdaughter and turned around and shot himself. Running away with her. He wanted to take her for his wife. And that was sad, but it was not Lore way. And for years that place been haunted.

Well, in life they say a horse can see things before human being. They like dogs. Dogs can see what's in the wind. Well, horses are like that. When he got to this corner of this place, a farm, it was dark, just coming into dark from twilight; clear as anything he could see these two people coming towards him. Well, the horse just went up. Never turned over or nothing. And they was going around. All of a sudden, he said, there was this white lady come from nowhere, grabbed the reins of that horse and just led that horse straight through. Went two miles up the road, looked back and nothing was there. When he got there, he sort of come back to his senses, he knew that was his mother.

She protected him right home. He was dark bloke, but when he come back, he was white as a wadjala. He turned white with a fright. And he reckoned, 'No, I'll never go through there no more, not on a horse and cart.' Spirits of these people. I said they must have a restless soul. I see a lot of people like that in my travels. This might be one of my gifts, too. Feel a hatred that someone don't like you, especially if they got eyes. That's the danger. You've got to be very careful, very careful. Either that thing can grab you, take you down with it or you can even feel it going. I find that all the time. I hear lots of spirits like that, yet I know the family is very cheeky and fight all the time, but they haven't got the hatred much. They express their hate straight out, but they not dangerous people. But the spirits might be, the ones with the eyes, like years ago when I had an experience with Mum.

Uncle Malcolm, my mother's brother come up to me: 'Now little girl, it's time to slow down,' he said. 'From now on you going to be living here with us gang, here on the reserve. No more wadjala way.' I was stuck in a barrier. Looking around, how am I going to do my life? What am I going to do with myself? And it was so hard, getting used to two sides of life. 'Sit down,' he said. I had to sit down and he'd tell me everything about my family, who my mother was and my father.

Then I found I had another family to get used to. Go to Esperance on holidays. Show off and all – I was terrible for that. They said, 'Slow down little girl. We're your own cousins.' What? How come? 'Your mother and father, that's my Uncle and Auntie. You learn to respect your family.' I was thinking these fellas sound like the mob in Gnowangerup. I thought I better not say too much to them. They say: 'Slow down little girl. You're still learning Noongar. That's your culture.' Do I have to? 'You have to all right. Get it into your head before you get any older so you can tell your grannies when the time comes.' I respected that. I thought, sometime in my life I have to slow down because I used to look around me and the girls, younger than me and about my age and I couldn't understand, they was like they was stuck between two cultures.

Then, all the girls my age who come through Gnowangerup with me, I'm thinking are they getting fat all of a sudden? Used to go to my old Auntie. How come they big fat people? 'You don't know nothing, little girl,' she used to say. 'You don't know nothing. You know you saw your Mum like that for Hilary and Russell?' Yeah. 'That's what's happening. They all pregnant.' And girls my own age I grew up with, you know? Oh yuck, I'm not going to be like that. No way. And I looking round I went to my cousin, she wasn't well herself. You fellas all getting too fat. 'Go away little girl,' they said. 'We having babies!' What? But you fellas same age or younger than me! That's one thing that stuck in my head all them times. Oh, I'm not going to be like that. I'm getting a job. Go round the corner and look here, my niece, boodjari one walking along. Boodjari, that means when you're pregnant. And old Auntie reckon, 'Don't you get like that. We'll chase you out of Gnowangerup if we see you like this.' And that was good for me, because I remember she used to tell me things like that. If I was in the wrong, I ask her and she'll explain it to me.

Uncle Malcolm Roberts, he was an old champion for me. He was my strength. He really used to explain things to me. Real fatherly. A lovely man. My Mum was his youngest sister. He told me a lot. 'You my girl, my favourite niece. You my baby sister's daughter, Ing. You the only Ing we got. I want you to listen to me. You can't live that life forever. That's Mission life. You got to come our way. I'll tell you things that are already happening to you,' in a real old powerful man way. He was a powerful old man. Them days they called them like doctor man. He knew everything about life. What's going to happen, how it's going to happen. For years, I've been trying to work that out. I think he's been giving me some too, because I get the same way now. I can see things before it happens. He always told me you my favourite. 'Do the right thing in life. Don't be like them other girls.' I said what you mean? Him and his old wife said, 'Look at them. They've all got little ones now, their little babies.' That never worried me.

And I really trusted him. Only one, him and my Auntie, two Aunties, they sort of helped me right through what I was going through. They were there for me. I guess I was lucky to have them in my life because if I didn't have them, I might have been in and out of jail now. There was just something stopping me from getting that far. I'd get up and walk away from it. And I thank my Elders for that.

Getting to know my family was very frightening. I didn't know what they do and I didn't know how to do it. I knew a lot about my Mum and Dad but my brother didn't know them. And I have to be good to tell my sister and brother. They was still in Marribank, Carrolup. My cousin, Rita Dempster, she knew I was coming from a different life at the Mission and would find it very hard on the reserve. She spoke to a wonderful woman that I already knew from the Mission, Miss Blunt. She was a single lady then. She was one of the missionaries and she had a house in Gnowangerup. I asked her if she could get me a job somewhere. I don't want to live on the reserve. She said, 'The reserve is not for you. You come and make your bed home at my place until I can find a job for you.' I stayed with Miss Blunt for about a month, but on the weekends, I went back to the reserve and stayed with Rita and her husband, Jackie so I could slowly fit in with people on the reserve. They had seven kids and I used to look after them when I was there.

And when I went home to the reserve on the weekend, they had all them old ladies. Auntie Maggie Williams, she was beautiful. Big old lady she was. Big, solid built lady. She was my mother's half sister. She was a Coyne before she married a Williams. She was a Dab, but they was all sort of like first cousins and that, so they were sisters and brothers like we are now to my family. That was a good time. She told me everything about Mum. She said: 'You know, girl, you looking more like your mother every time I see you. They should have named you Tilda.' I woke up then, I thinking, hey, I must have looked like me Mummy. I used to go around every camp and have a yarn with all my old aunties. Big mob on the reserve. Must be about 50 families. And oh, good fun. Yeah. You join in everybody else's company, yarning. I must have been about sixteen at that stage.

Singing along with all the old people. It brings back lots of good memories. Look back now and it's all there. For they will be forever in our lives. But that's a memory I wouldn't want to cut off from, a memory I want to tell how my heart feels today. It's for my own gang. I want to tell them that I did that. And that's the best part of my years, I think. I needed something like that to grow up. For years, I was like the spoilt one. And my brother, my brothers, they knew what I was. Old cousins, first cousins. In our family our first cousins is our brothers and sisters and their mothers, we have to call them Mum. And the aunties are usually all the second cousins. They our cousins, the second cousins. But the first cousins, was our sisters and brothers. Because that's your mother's sister and your father's brother and your mother's brother. I learnt that very quick. But I had good aunties in Gnowangerup. Aunties who'd really tell me. I'd ask them where's my mother? What she look like?

'You should look at yourself sometime' or 'You look at yourself in the mirror when you're combing your hair next time. You looking at your mother's face. You same.'

My old Auntie at the reserve, old Chinese lady, Auntie Mary Woods. Beautiful old lady. Spot on. I'm glad I had legends. Lonely girl, she used to call me. I was her pet. She used to walk leaning over and head twisted over to the side, shake her head, whole body shake all the time. She say, 'I feel like going to the cemetery today.' I used to walk right around with her in the bush to the cemetery, look at all the graves of family. Walk her home. 'Don't go girl.' I'd sit down, have a rest with her, make her a cup of tea and a sandwich or something. Then everybody used to come home. 'Don't go for long, girl, my lonely girl.' Joyce, her daughter used to say to me: 'You're her daughter. That's your mother there.' Ah, I thinking there was two lovely mums with me all the time. I ask her: Is she with me all the time? 'Your mother, she always there for you.'

I had a lot of white friends. Some I talk to over the years. They say, 'Hello, Helen' in a pleasant kind of way. And yet, the reserve Noongars say: 'Ugh, look at that! How come you can talk to everybody?' 'Ah, she wadjala herself. She's a Mission girl. She can get away with anything.' I really didn't like that. Time for me to get out, start pulling my own weight in life instead of relying on everybody else. I had a brother to keep, and a sister. They be looking for me one day.

7

Work

SO, DURING THE week I stayed with Miss Blunt until she got me a job in the Gnowangerup Hospital. And that was good, only it was haunted, that hospital. You see things going where you would never believe it. This one was very creepy. Walk through the passageway and these people come to you out of nowhere. All I can do is run. You not allowed to scream where all them sick people are. I held my breath until I got outside and then I screamed. They knew when I was around. I was running away from something. I lived at the hospital and learnt to be a nurse's aide. I was the only Noongar there, really. Florence come for a little while, my cousin, but she left and I was sort of on my own. I didn't mind. I grew up with wadjalas. I knew wadjala ways. Sometimes I wore a uniform – if I felt like it. Red and white or blue and white, same as any other hospital, but we was special, us mob. Never wore a cap. I didn't like it. Mine never used to stay on, anyway. Sometimes when we dress up till people come and see us, like a doctor come in, 'Ah, Helen, you look nice today.' Then he'll say, 'Well, I'm going now, so you can take it off.' And the quicker it's off, the better.

I guess I was lucky. It was just like something up there was looking after me. Mum. Granted me a little bit of pleasure and pushing me on, as if to say this is your life, girl. I had good training. I didn't mind learning all the first aid and mothercraft. I passed that with flying colours. So I was good at something. In a way I was pleased because I learnt to be a housewife and mother and housekeeper. Over the years I learnt a lot more about cooking. I done it all myself.

I wasn't there for long, six months, or five months. I wanted the freedom, and that was the best part, but also I wanted a refuge to get used to the reserve and there was no better way than the hospital. Getting used to life away from the Mission. That was good. I was one of Matron Johnson's special workers. And all through my life was like that.

I seen a lot of these kids that are young man and woman now. Got children of their own. Seen them born. Nursed them in my arms when they was babies. Put their little cheek next to mine. And I was taught, 'That's your nephew.' 'I'm your sister.' My cousins used to come and tell me, 'We one blood, us family.' Well, that was good. I guess I was lucky. Really lucky. So, I stuck to my work in Gnowangerup Hospital. It used to be good. I learnt First Aid, how to be in mothercraft for the little children. Learnt all that.

Old Matron Johnson, she was a big old sister. She's a lovely old lady. She was like an Auntie to me. Gnowangerup was a real old hospital. And I used to go to her room, knock on the door of her apartment. Matron I can't sleep in my room. Never miss, about nine o'clock in my room that door would automatically open by itself, because from where the front door was it lead straight down to the hospital. On this side was the morgue. Noongar sleeping there? That's the most awfullest thing out. Another time I went to get a drink of water from the fridge. This old lady standing in the middle of the passageway and I don't know what time it was, about two or three o'clock in the morning. And she's standing there and she's smiling at me and coming towards me. I just turned and screamed. Well, I must have woke all of the hospital up. Poor sick people. This white girl she come out, 'What's the matter?' I told her I saw that dead woman coming towards me! 'No, she's dead. I see the same woman.' Well that was it! I'm not going to work here. Too haunted. And another old man he be standing there doing something near his bed. This is all dead people. Spirits, ghosts. And you'd ask them what you doing out of bed? Tell them jump into bed. Look around again and they gone. But they were harmless. You shouldn't be frightened of the dead. Be frightened of a live person if you was frightened of anything.

Matron, poor old sister, Matron Johnson, standing there freezing cold in winter. 'What's the matter, Helen, dear?' Tell her, 'You know there's a spooky ghost here and I don't like it.

She comes out in the damnedest places. She seems to watch me everywhere I go.' 'Well, she must like you, Helen. That's something to be proud of. You pick your mattress up and come and sleep in my room on the floor there.' Which I did and I had the most loveliest sleep. When I was frightened, I was allowed to do that. And the white girls used to come there, 'You sleeping in the matron's room.' 'Oh, she don't mind. She walks around me and goes to her bed.' 'How come? We try that she'll tell us to go home. Helen, you could get away with anything.' I used to have a good sleep.

I made some good friends when I was at school and then later working in Gnowangerup Hospital. Rosemary Freeguard, she's married now. We still have a yarn, talk about life. Helen Franton, Julie Cockran. We all old grandmothers now, happily married. I see them from time to time. They all come from the town of Gnowangerup, all wadjalas. I had a lot of these friends like that. Shirley MacDougall, she was my little sister, wadjala way. She was little, tinier than us. I used to look after her. Marilyn Freeguard, she's Rosemary's little sister. Betsy Buchanan, we got close over the years, me and Betts. I can make friends with white girls, but they will not go towards people from the reserve. Even the Noongars now looking, 'You know 'em?' I say, 'Yeah, we used to go to school together.' And they say, 'You the only one they talk to.' And I look back and I say, 'I'm thankful I had the time in the Mission. I can do things where my family couldn't. Soon as they do something, they get into trouble for it.'

And they'll say, 'Oh no, Helen don't do things like that.' But that was a very prejudiced town, you can only say hello.

Lot of Noongar kids all born there at Gnowangerup Hospital. One treasure I knew that was born at the Gnowangerup Hospital was my nephew. A special little boy. His mother, my sister, my first cousin, was having him when I hadn't been there long. I keep asking my other aunties, Is Maudie in yet? 'Yeah, she come in. She's probably in that first ward.' I went there. Yeah, she was there. She's sitting there, 'I'm in pain.' And I'm thinking, yeah? So I rub her back. Take a deep breath I keep saying to her. I don't know nothing about this. And my first cousin and I used to go and take her biscuits or sandwiches, because she was my sister. She'd save it for her husband. He used to plough all the wheat fields around. Good worker too, hard worker. Anyway, she come in and had her baby, and she named him, this little boy. And I seen him born and was the first to hold him. Picked him up and put his little cheek next to mine. He's my baby – Toono. His name is Sandy Brown. Toono, that's his Noongar name. Little one. That's my treasure baby. My GN-dot baby. GN-dot was short for Gnowangerup. Geraldton was just GN without a dot.[3] It was a big joke. Toono was my mothercraft baby. First baby. I loved that little boy. I loved him, cuddled him, hugged him. It feels like

---

3 Western Australian vehicle number-plating system, which identifies regional districts.

centuries ago now. And he grew up into a beautiful big boy. When he was a young man, he used to come and see me all the time. I was his favourite Mum. He'd tell everybody with pride, 'That's my favourite Mum.'

Got in trouble over the years with the law. Never seen him for a long time. Got married for a little while, took off and left a woman. Then he got into trouble big time and done all them years in jail. But he always used to come home and see me. He died in Geraldton. I think he just collapsed. He was a good boy. They brought him back home to his Mum and Dad. Father's still going. His mother died. When he died, well we had his funeral home in Gnowangerup Baptist Church. He was flown back from Geraldton. My niece up there paid for it. She rang and told me, 'You know Mum, we're going to have Toono's funeral home in Gnowangerup.' She asked me first and I said you make sure you come home.

He was my mothercraft baby. I was the first one to hold him. He was my little treasure. Now I'm laying him down to bury him at home. And at the church a lot of people was there, all family like, young fellas. Well, I got up, went up on the platform. I said, can I say something, Brother Albert? And after all the tears and that, I said you know, this little boy, my Toono, Sandy Brown. I was in the hospital when he was born, working at the Gnowangerup Hospital. He was my first baby I held before anybody else, even Brother Morris. And I put his cheek on the side of mine and I done the same to him when he was in his coffin. Now I'm putting my baby down to rest. And it was a strange kind of feeling came all over me. I just felt as if I needed to say it. Thank you for giving me a little bit of pleasure, coming here, putting you to rest next to your mother. And like I talking to him, everybody just went quiet. You couldn't hear a pin drop. I took his cheek and put it right on the side of mine. He was my baby. That really hurt.

That's when I cried. I don't cry for him now, he's laughing, he's with Harry John, him and Harry John, two brothers, my son. They don't want to listen to all this. Put a smile on your face. They together now, they brothers, my two boys. After that, I just got up and walked out. I looked back. Poor fellas, don't know what they crying for. He needed that to be said. But that's how I felt for him. Everybody looked at me and started smiling. All the young fellas that knew him was there. But he was my baby.

8

The wisdom of Uncle Malcolm

AFTER I FINISHED at the Gnowangerup Hospital I went back to live on the reserve with my Uncle Malcolm and Auntie Bonnie. She was a dear old duck. She had one teeth in the front, big old teeth and she'll sit down sucking on this thing all the time, her little grandson on the side sucking on a dummy in his mouth. It was the funniest sight out. I'll say to Uncle Malcolm, get her teeth out, she sounds funny. 'Ah, you be like this one day,' she said. I beat her – I got no teeth now. Uncle Malcolm, he wasn't a big fella, about the same as my Dad. His hair was jet black with grey in it, a little bit wavy. He used to tie it back in a ponytail sometimes. Sometimes he had a beard and other times his face was clean. He was the dominant figure in my life. Right through my life of growing up, he was always telling me what I should do, shouldn't do.

Uncle Malcolm always used to tell me things. I'd look at him. How this old man know? How you know, Uncle? One time he telling me, 'Come here girl, sit down.' Me and him looking up at the clouds. 'Look up there,' he said. And this cloud come from nowhere. 'That's wara, something going to happen. That's what I want you to do, when I tell you anything you watch the clouds. They'll always tell you in the cloud of anything happening around you. Or a dead branch off a tree, that's wrong – wara. Yeah, you could be sitting down and say you in the bush this side under the shade, and if that limb fall off that tree, fall down on the ground in front of you, you got to get a little dry bush or stick, and hit it only three times and it'll break the curse from it. That mean death, you going to lose someone, so if you can hit it before it go dry, you right. Just takes that curse away, whatever it is. That's a terrible feeling. But after you did it, you right. Worst part of it if you don't know how long it had been there. But if you see it first hand, that's the time to hit him three times, no more. That's how things used to happen them days. It'll break that curse. Little things like that you can see things around you. Noongars had powerful way like that. Wongis do too. Over the years I've learnt there's always something there telling you don't do that, don't go there. You'll know a lot.' And that's how I got my knowledge. Auntie Bonnie always saying to me I'm his favourite. 'Silly old man, I love him,' sucking on her one tooth.

I come back a bit late one day. My Uncle, he said to me, 'You not on your own.' He had sent me down to get two loaves of bread, with my cousin Moono to go company with me. He was a bit older than me. So I went and got talking to everybody down there and forgot about the bread. Anyway, I realised I had to take this bread home, so went and got two loaves. We coming through the bush dusk time, just on sunset, singing along, me and my cousin, Moono. And he used to be very scared; every little shadow, he'd run – take off like John Landy. Leave anybody behind.

Well, something rattled in the bush. And I sung out to Moono to wait there. He never waited. He bolted! He had emu in his legs. He was an emu that day. Thick bush, and I come walking along by myself and Uncle Malcolm stood up looking over the fire. He was a little short fella, wavy black hair with grey. He was solid. Very shy. Him and my Auntie looked the same. 'Oh,' he said, 'that's you!' 'Yeah, why? You sent me for couple of loaves of bread for these little kids.' He said, 'Where that boy? Why wasn't he walking with you?' I said, 'No, he left me for dust, Dad.' And Uncle Malcolm, he reckon, 'I'm going to tell him off when I sees him again. I know Moono weren't there with you. We seen him past us like a bullet.' He sat down and he said, 'You'll know one day little girl. Look at me.' and I looked at him. 'What happened? You okay? Were you on your own?' I says, 'Yes.' But old people, they can see signs and things that I can't. He said, 'I'd better look at you.' He could see my mother and my father with me, their spirits. 'Yeah,' he said, 'That's right. There was three of you. Three! One too close to you.' He told me my mother was getting too close to me. He was boss. I said, 'No, Uncle Malcolm, no one was walking with me.

Moono took off and left me standing in the bush over there!' 'No, there was three of you coming out. That's your mother and your father. They getting too close to you. I think Mum's a bit too dangerous. She is very strong in spirit. I think she wants you with her. They still got eyes, spirit eyes. I'll check you over. Come back tomorrow and I'll check you over.'

So, I went to my Auntie's and stayed there with her. Come back next day and he said, 'You right now?' 'I couldn't go to sleep last night, Uncle Malcolm.' And he said, 'You know, I'll tell you straight out now your mother, she'll always be there for you but now she is too close to you.' Sitting out and I'm talking to Uncle Malcolm. Auntie Bonnie asleep and all the kids. And he says, 'You think we on our own?' I said, 'I know you now, Dad, you not playing fiddlesticks with me.' And he said, 'Don't be frightened. Look at that fire.' This little coal kept coming out, going back by itself. He says, 'There's somebody here with us. Don't get frightened. You know what that is? That'd be your father or your mother. They're too close to you.' So, he done something – Noongar ways he put his hands. 'Lie down,' he said. So, I lay down. I laid for one full day, but all I can hear is this funny, terrible noise. He rubbing me all over my head. Noongar medicine. I remember going to sleep. Having the best sleep, but I could still hear this terrible noise, like she was fighting him, her spirit, like she was wrestling with something and trying to say get away, get away, that's my baby. Something like that, but she never said it but it was like a fight there. My Uncle put the ashes, done something to her eyes, burnt spirit eyes out. Dad's eyes out. That's how strong he was, him and my Auntie. He caught Mum's spirit. And after that he was washing his hands; must have woke me.

She telling me afterwards, 'Your mother getting too close to you. Old boy was a bit worried about you be the next one to go.' That's how they work, old Noongars. And she said, 'She was getting a bit too close, so your Uncle fixed you up. You be right now.' I said, 'Hey, Auntie Bonnie, any tea?' 'Oh yeah, here, same place as you left it.' 'Where I went to?' 'You was nookert – asleep,' she said. 'Your Uncle put you to sleep until he was ready to wake you. You be right now. Your Uncle, he told me that.' Ever since that I never seen no one tell me thing like that. No one. Because my Uncle he was an old doctor man.

You know what he said to me? 'Your Mummy always with you but she was getting too close to you. Little bit longer she might have took you home with her.' Take my spirit or something – put me to sleep and that would have been it. And I believe that very, very much and I'm glad that I experienced it.

Uncle Malcolm was special to me. He was there when no one was around. My mother was his younger sister and it was his job to tell me. He used to teach me what spirit things to look out for. He knew things before it happens. He could see in the clouds, by birds. Sometimes we used to just sit by the fire and he'd say to me, 'You'll know in time, my girl, you'll know one day what this life going to hold for you and that's going to make you big and strong for your Mum and Dad and all us old fellas. When things come to you, you'll know what I'm talking about. You'll know when the time comes that you going the right way and I hope you learn before it's too late. You got to be a strong lady. I won't be around for that. That's way down there – in the future. Now, I tell you so you know what to look out for. Sit down, my girl, I'm going to teach you things.'

I didn't know at the time but after a while I sort of worked things out. He'd tell me to look out for signs in the sky. Even now, I can see things in the weather. He taught me that. Anything that look funny up there, you know there's something going to happen or you going to lose one of your family. I know that deep down in my heart. I think that'll always stay with me. If anybody dead, you see that balyat, he's shaped like a grave in the sky. This is the thing for death. And you'll pick the sand up, you have to do that and chuck towards this balyat and tell it go away, go away, not here: it'll go away, looking for somewhere else to go. Creepy, but it's there. You see that cloud, just black. If it's anyone close to our family it'll come there and you know what that is. Wara, no good. You're not taking our family. And that sort of brought me through life. And people always say, 'How you know?' I say, 'I been taught.' I said to Uncle Malcolm, 'All right if I can use it?' He said, 'You the main one, I'm giving this to you.' Uncle Malcolm, his wisdom is still there. At the time I didn't think of it much, but after I went back to him and I said to him, 'You know Uncle Malcolm, I love you. You Mummy's brother.' You can't find another special love like that. I must have been a mad person sometimes, but I listened to my main old uncles and aunties. So I know they doing that for me for the best to look after me, so I can be able to look after the little fellas.

See, by then I was finished my job at the hospital. I wanted to get in with my family before I get any older, so that's when my old Uncle told me everything. Who was who and what was what. My aunties, they told me everything. 'You, you our blood. Slow down, you're not a wadjala girl any more. You Noongar. You got to learn to live like a Noongar.' That hurt. I think that pushed me to be more stubborn, never used to like being told. And that was the hardest time in my life, getting used to two cultures. Trying to live a Noongar way, but you got this wadjala way in the background. You are who you are. I used to sit down and temper up. They reckon, 'It's not your fault. Not your fault. You got to come and pull our way a little bit. But you're strong minded, you like your old Auntie, strong-minded old lady and that's what's going to bring you through life.' Uncle Malcolm taught me how to be Noongar. I used to tell Russell the things that Uncle Malcolm taught me, but Hilary was too little to understand.

I never used to listen, only to Uncle Malcolm and my mother's sister, old Ridlan Williams. She was Ridlan Roberts

Dab before she got married; after that she was Ridlan Williams. Sister Rita was always telling me what to do. I finished with that. I'd find a way to sneak out, don't come back till early next morning. Go and have a time with the girls and a broom waiting on us when we get back. I used to be a little leader because all the girls used to follow me around. Even when they was finishing high school I used to go to another town and who should pop up but the girls from Gnowangerup. I say you girls you getting me in trouble. 'Oh, we like it with you, Auntie.'

Rosie, she was my best mate. We was in the same class in school together. We the same age, she never forgets to tell me that. I was the outlaw – the devil lady. Auntie Grace would say, 'Now Ing, why don't you behave yourself. Don't teach Rosie bad habits.' Run away. Two oldies would come to Perth to pick me up. I didn't know nothing about Perth. Anyone could have knocked me in the head up here. I didn't know where's where, who's who. Take me back home. 'Now listen little girl, you sit down and you listen to me. Old Mum getting old now. Me too. We can't go up and down to pick you up. Our old mate be moving from Gnowangerup soon, the Welfare man. He won't be around. And every time you go on to anywhere, we got to go and pick you up. Me, I don't mind that. You my girl, you my sister's daughter. You listen to me now.' Well, he used to tell me things. He used to turn around and say to me, 'You know, my girl, in time you'll know what's been happening but there's a lot of things that

I couldn't tell you but you'll find out for yourself.' And that's just what I'm doing now.

Little bit later, when I was in my twenties, old Uncle Malcolm and Auntie Bonnie took me to Bremer Bay with them for Easter Holiday. Numby, Hazel's husband, took us down there. That's his Noongar name, Numby. All my little grandnieces and that, they all like little steps and ladders. I used to help them. Their little girl, Dianne, was a baby then. He said, 'You know what, my girl, I don't have to fish. Look at all these people standing with all the lines. Just stand back, watch them girls so they won't go in the sea. Where Auntie Bonnie?' I said she making a fire for us. So, we're all sitting down watching Pop. And he said to me, 'Stand back my girl.' What you doing, Dad? 'Come back here,' Auntie Bonnie said, 'Come and sit back with me.' And he told us all to sit on this sandbank and watch what he's doing. So, I was sitting down. He grabbed this big, dry stick from nowhere and him and his other grandson went out, pants tucked up and beard swaying. Dry bush and he hit that water. He hit that seawater one, two, three times. Stood back; us kids up and down, standing, sitting, standing. 'Don't worry' he said. 'Sit down. We don't have to fish. We don't need no fishing rods. They'll come directly.'

All the kids standing there, looking. And true, put the stick on the side, waited until it dry out and threw it in the fire and burnt it up. He says, 'Now sit down, sit down all you little fellas. Look out there in the ocean.' Oh, it was a beautiful day. Hey! Look there! I could see a dolphin chucking something up in the air. Porpoise chucking all them salmon up in the air, bringing them in to shore. I seen that happen! Old fella, he knew what he was doing. That thing just come right in to shore, just right to the place where these little kids couldn't go too much in the deep. We running out and pulling salmon in! And skippy, big skippy and tailor! You only just take as much as you want. Don't be greedy.

And that was the biggest excitement in my life. We standing looking, look at all the porpoises playing with the big salmon and herring and skippy and that! They bringing them right in to us. Right there. All the fish. Porpoise swimming around jumping around us. The porpoise, they're like dolphins. They look at you as if they know you. You could see it in their eyes. And these big fish coming in and we grabbing them. 'Only take two, that's enough. That'll do us. Feed all the kids.' Uncle Malcolm! He said, 'You'll never starve, long as you have the sense to get a boy or man to hit that water, just three times.' And it was like that porpoise they knew old Noongar way, watching, 'Oh, they had enough. Let's take it out again.' And then they gone. And Uncle Malcolm say, 'Woman not allowed to do this. It's only us man or young man coming into his teenage life, he can do it.' That's why I sit and I listen. Now, I can't do it, no woman can't do it but my Uncle showed me. When he hit that seawater, because down there our way our old people, they come with the ocean. Beautiful country. And that belongs to all the old people. And he was like he was watching us, that ocean.

We said to Uncle Malcolm, we all hungry here. He say, 'You got your fish.' All the kids all lined up, 'Look at my fish. Don't touch my fish!' He taught me that's the best way. 'Bush tucker here. Clean that old guts out.' I say to Uncle Malcolm, you do it. He cut it down, open it. I cleaned it out, washed it in the seawater. 'That's the best,' he reckon. 'Leave a little bit of seawater in it. Put a pigface in there.' Pretty pink and yellow flowers, bany. Dip them in the seawater first. He stuffed them all where the guts was, maybe put an onion or garlic in, wrap up in paperbark, all wet, put them in the ashes, and leave them there. How he done that paperbark – pure white, beautiful, soft fish. And oh, you could smell it. It was beautiful. I never taste fish like that. Noongars tell me how they could cook fish. My old Auntie taught me how to cook it Noongar way. And I can do it. And all the little kids had their one little fish.

I said to Uncle Malcolm how you know the ocean like that? 'That's old Noongar there. That's our family. He know us. We all went through these waters. That's one thing you have to learn down here. Instead of sitting down all day with a fishing line, we do it the easy way. Our family in the ocean too, especially in Bremer Bay. Oh, that sea knows, knows your blood. As soon as you're a stranger there you see the waves coming up high.' My Uncle Malcolm said, 'You see there, we've got a stranger with us, my old brother up there from Moora. The sea don't know him.' Ah, I tell you it's marvellous! You stand there and look at that and all of a sudden; a wave will come to your foot. Stranger here. When he come and sit with us, Uncle Malcolm would talk to that ocean and that ocean will just get calm. And you can see it all happening in the front of you. I never, ever dreamt I'll ever see that sort of thing done.

Them kids are grandmothers themselves now, that they used to look after. Out of all the family, they only know me. Nanny Ing, that's Nanny Ing used to come and stay with us. I was young and stupid in them days but I had to look after the little ones. I'm thankful about that. That's one thing I always had in my blood was taking care of children.

And way around the other side, Cape Le Grand is beautiful. They can put a show on there. The beauty around it. They knows you family. You know when you're with family. Soon as any stranger go there, rough as anything. I seen that happen. And he reckon, 'That's all our family there.' The mystery that that old man taught me. I look back now and I say thank you, Uncle. You got me there. Maybe that's why I'm older and wiser. And I wouldn't want to be anywhere else. A lot of people don't understand that.

I'd love to take my husband, Orly, down that way. Be solid. This my old people's country. It's a beautiful, spiritual thing. I'll ask these old fellas would he be allowed to do it, maybe, because we older now. We might be able to. I think he would, if I picked the right bush and he can do it. I'll tell him just sit down now watch what Uncle Malcolm done. But I have to tell the ocean first, that's old Noongar right through here. Watch all the families down there. If that ocean know you a stranger you can see them waves all getting rough on the rocks. Water just automatically goes over. You can't fish there. No wadjalas can fish. Get the odd smart one, get drowned. Can't be told. You don't do that, not down Bremer. Very powerful, there. Oh, I'd love to take you down there. I'll take you walk along the beach and you can feel the presence. That old ocean watching you like you family.

When my niece got married, she wanted to go to Bremer Bay. I said you be very careful down there, that's our family there. You look after our family and he'll look after you, old grandfather, he's like the boss. He never dies. He's always watching out for our family, our ocean. He knows, he can feel my heart. It's a beautiful thing, true. Uncle Malcolm always tell me always come down and say hello, that's all our family. He look after us if we look after him. You respect him and he'll give us everything. I tell my grannies the same. I know that since I've grown up a bit.

My Auntie Grace, she said to me, she a big old fat lady. She said I had a cold of flu or something. And she reckon, 'You know the best thing for you, girl?' She said to her son, 'Barney, take me down to the beach, front beach.' 'What for? You can't get away from them waves.' We used to have fun with her. 'And no,' she said, 'I got Ing, got a cold here.' Told Barney and them go along, walk that way somewhere. 'Take all your clothes off,' she said. No, go away I said to her. No. 'Take it all off, leave your petticoat on. Now run and jump in that sea. I'm sick of you lying back with the flus and that.' So, I run and jumped clean in that ocean. It was that warm on the ocean. Lovely and warm. I didn't want to get out. 'Come on, that's enough.' That thing then, whatever it was just went from me. Next day I was climbing a tree, riding a horse. Barney reckon, 'Old fellas. That's medicine.'

Russell, he used to say to me, 'I never had that talking with old people that you had.' I said you know why? Because you were stubborn like George Nellie, stubborn. You never talk to people. You always, 'What they talking to me for?' type of thing. Knock them over. Very stubborn. 'What about yourself?' he say to me. I got Mum's heart, you got Dad's heart. You'll always be like that. But I'll always be there for you, baby brother. He used to hate that. 'I'm not a baby anymore. I'm a young man.' I say you'll always be my baby. You my Tow Tow. Used to be on that baking powder tin, Cream of Tartar. Noongars call it Tow Tow. They couldn't read it properly, that's how he got that name. He was a terrible tasting kid. He said, 'Mum used to call me that.' You can remember that? He was a little blonde-headed wrecker. Noongars making that damper there, they put Cream of Tartar in damper to make it rise in the ashes. Instead of Tartar they say Tow Tow.

Respect has been gone for years in Gnowangerup. That's why Uncle Malcolm said to me, 'I don't want you growing up here. Go away. Get out of this town. Get out of it. You might be married to your own brother or uncle. I don't want my family growing up like that.' Anyway, my old cousin, Rita, who was looking after me because I was still underage, moved to Albany, so I decided to move with her. When I was getting ready to go down to Albany with Rita and Jackie, Russell and Hilary were still in Carrolup then. Got to see them once a month. Got a lift – lots of family there that would take me. Or I might see them in Katanning. Russell, he was possessive as usual. Hilary used to call me Mummy. And I thinking ah, Mum's still here.

They was well cared for, but not as good as Gnowangerup. There was a lot of children's deaths there. I was frightened Russell and Hilary might get caught up on it, but they was okay. A lot of the kids was drowned or got burnt, burnt up. Even now when you sit outside in them old houses you can feel their presence. All of a sudden, you can hear little foots going running past you. I was scared as anything, I took straight for the door and even outside you could hear footsteps, clear as daylight. This was restless souls, that's how things are in Marribank. Even hear singing in that beautiful stone church, but nobody there. They wanted to go places but they was stuck there. And that's sad. When we did that documentary, you could feel the presence of people watching us. That's very strong in Marribank. Even daylight, sometimes you could be sitting in the kitchen waiting for the kettle to boil and a spoon will drop on the floor. Russell and Theresa would go outside and they were Christians. 'Eh, hold on, hold on Russell,' I'd say. 'Sit down and have a yarn with them. That's a restless soul. They don't know how to rest.' I couldn't stand Marribank Mission. Must have been terrible years ago. All I can feel is creepy bad feelings. I never stayed in that Mission but I could feel things that, you know, eww, it's an awful place. 'You'll know, you know,' Uncle Malcolm said. I could feel it. They want to tell us something but they can't, because we're no relation. That was sad.

And I used to say to the kids, 'Do you ever see things?' 'Yeah, all the time, sister, all the time,' older ones said. 'Woman in the kitchen helping you washing the dishes up, but she's got her own dishes. And then someone would come along like they was putting wood down on the floor. That's why I was always running away,' she said. 'I used to get in trouble for running away. And how was your Mission?' I tell her that was good. We had peace there in Gnowangerup.

So, then I lived on the Albany reserve. That was pretty good. I looked after the kids. Kept myself occupied. I was used to looking after kids. My little nieces and nephews, they wasn't easy. They used to get into mischief, but they used to follow me everywhere. I was like Mother Goose. My sister and brother-in-law are Christian people. Only Noongars I can really relate to back then, go tell my problems to. She had two elder brothers and I used to sit for hours yarning around the fire with them. They used to tell me things too. Another cousin just down the road; when I had enough of them, I'd go and ask her. This is how I got bits and pieces together about who I really am.

Stars are beautiful down south. Borden, Gnowangerup, Albany. Seven sister, there's a story there. They were sent away, old people up this end told me, to go and get men. But they didn't have to, because blokes used to come in and they take them, pretty one, you know? That was his woman. She wasn't allowed to go back home. And somewhere along the line they all met up together, run away because their men were too cruel to them. They went away that way somewhere. You see them all up there, all the sisters together standing, one little one behind. She must have been just out of the reach, but she's trying to catch them up. Mummy used to tell me that story long time. Auntie Ellie used to tell me that. She reckon must have been pretty Noongar woman, all got mans come down trying to get 'em all away from home, but no, they didn't like that sort of life, little kids most likely grew up and that and they all got lonely for each other and they went back home, looking around must be for the little sister, and she's there with them but she's not in with the main group. And they all got together, went home to their own country. That's where they's stationed, looking over us.

Southern Cross is a beautiful star. That's where we are. You know where you come from, south, right on the bottom, that's pointing homewards. I tell 'em up north and wherever I go, I got to go with the bottom one, take me home, Albany.

I got odd jobs around Albany. Stayed with wadjalas all over Albany. I had that many friends. The Aboriginal reserve in Borden had closed and we came and went between Albany and the Gnowangerup reserve and Perth. I had years of finding out who I was – me. That's a treasured time. And only old Uncle had the strength enough to tell me.

9

Hilary

AFTER GNOWANGERUP MISSION closed, Hilary and Russell went into Marribank but Hilary came up here in Perth from out of Marribank Mission. She must have been in her early teens. They were all running away from Marribank them days. They couldn't stay there anymore because it was too terrible. That's one Mission I wouldn't want her to be in. That was a horrible Mission.

Russell had only just left Carrolup Mission in Katanning. He was about seventeen, eighteen. They had a choice to leave the Mission and just go, if they like to travel. Well, the first choice was Esperance for most of our boys. Get away from Gnowangerup and Katanning. There was nothing down there going for them anyway. They grabbed the first one, on the bus to Esperance. Did farm work, driving the tractors, picking the weeds up. Once in a while I used to pop in and see how he's going, and that was the best part of going to Esperance.

ABOVE: Gnowangerup Mission. *Photo State Library of Western Australia number 134394PDM*

BELOW: Ing and Russell's father, George Nellie. *Photo courtesy of the Department of Indigenous Affairs, Aboriginal History Research Unit*

Gnowangerup Mission. Drawings by Ing Nellie — Entrance, Shop, Church, House with garden

ABOVE: Gnowangerup Mission. Drawing by Ing Nellie, House with swing.

BELOW: Ing, Dolly Yorkshire and Rona Williams. The truck in the background transported Ing to the Mission when she was five years old.

ABOVE: Ing's sister Hilary, at far left of picture, at Gnowangerup Mission.

Photo State Library of Western Australia number 134349PD

BELOW: Ing's sister Hilary, left, at Gnowangerup Mission.

Photo State Library of Western Australia number134352PD

ABOVE: Russell Nellie

BELOW: Albert Knapp, Ing and Russell Nellie with a photo of George Nellie behind them.

ABOVE: Ing with her son, Harry John Nellie

BELOW: Ing raised Anthony from aged one week

ABOVE: Two watercolours by Ing

Ing. *Photo by Henry Kordas*

And Hilary, she stayed in Lane Street in Perth. That was a place where all the Noongar girls used to get to when they got no place to live. It was a Catholic home. Father O'Brien. He was a good old Father. He was a good old man. He knew us all, you know. We were all like his girls. And she was there for a while before I realised where she was. And they said, 'Your sister there, she'll be in the park soon.' I was told to go and pick her up and bring her back to where I was staying. No worries, I didn't mind that. So, I go through the park and I see her there. She was living rough at that time. 'Ah my Mummy, where you come from? That's my big sister,' she said to others. When I was around she behaved herself. She treated me like Mum. I'm the boss. I made that pretty clear to her. I told her, 'Come on, you coming home with me to Cabramatta Street in Ashfield. I got a house for you and Russell.' Three-bedroom little house.

One day they sitting around playing cards and I was cooking apple cake. I said to them, 'Now you two watch that cake in that stove for me. I'm going to go and have a shower.' I said to Russell, 'You listening? Watch this apple cake for me. You love apple cake and I got cream and all.' 'Aah, lovely, sister, lovely. You boss.' I must have been in there five minutes, ten minutes. When I come out, I smell this awful stinking smell. Burnt apple, burnt sugar. It was making me sick! When I come back in the kitchen, it was just black with smoke and the smoke was coming out of the oven. Turned the oven off and I look for those two people that should have been looking after that cake, but they was outside on the side of the road, sitting down. I stood there waving the mop at them. 'You come back here, you getting this.' They run up the hill. I yell, 'You better run.' I don't know where they went that day.

They went into town, telling everybody what happened at home. Tell everybody I drove them out. I didn't do that, they ran off themselves. But I caught them when they come back. Huh, big shots. 'Never again will you eat anything I cook. I'll save a little piece, that's good enough for you.' 'Hey, sister,' Russell say, 'I'm your favourite brother.' 'Me too, I'm your little sister,' say Hilary. I tell them, 'You both got the same Nellie mind. Laziness in your mind. You don't know what it is to get up and do it. You expect me to do it.' 'Yeah, but you're our big sister.' What can you say? I just feel like choking them, banging their heads together. They reckon, 'We got the best sister in the world. You like our Mum.' Even now I'm sure I can taste burnt apple. Must have burnt my tongue.

They ended up staying with me for nearly six months, but after that Hilary went her own way. Later I lived in Langford, then in Bassendean. And I think one day a long time ago when I went into Perth I looked and I said to my other cousin, 'You know what? I'm sure that looks like Hilary there.' Aah, she run. 'My big sister.' It was her, all right. But even then, she never told me about the two children she had.

Russell, he went to jail and Hilary, she got in jail with some other girls and that. I think she was a naughty girl somehow; she was always fighting with someone. I had left

Kalgoorlie by then and was down in Albany when they told me she was in the lockup when she died. 'She what? She got her own place.' 'No, she died in Perth in the lockup.' I think her polio had bit to do with it, but I think there was a bit of rough treatment there from this bloke she used to live with. I never used to like him. She wanted to come with me before but he wouldn't let her come. So, something happened in there. I think he might have got one or two of his sisters to give her a hiding in jail. She must have been 23 when she died. And that was how my little sister came to leave me. But she's still there in my heart. Always there.

They said in the jail they didn't think she had any family. They was just going to bury her how she was. Then Russell went in first. He said, 'No, that's my baby sister. I'm Russell Nellie. That's my youngest sister. We got a big sister yet to come up from Albany. And we want her to go back home to where her Mum and Dad is, in Gnowangerup.' Then I got up here and I told them, 'We want her body to be going back to Gnowangerup. I'm her elder sister.' So, I think it was $500.00. Took her back home. The family done it for us. And she was not far from Mum and Dad. We was able to bury her home in Gnowangerup. And that's my Hilary. She was my little sister. I felt empty after that, but I was old enough to understand then. Really get on with my living.

It was years after; long after she died I found out she had these two little girls. They were adopted out. I was already back from my travels around Australia and home in Albany when I found out about them, but I didn't know where I'd catch up with them. That's a sad, sad time. I didn't know she even had children until they was telling me Hilary had two daughters. Someone come and explained it to me, told me, 'Your sister got two children.' I said, 'What?' She had never said nothing to me about it. Hilary always wanted to do her own thing. Not long ago I said to Russell, 'You know what, brother? She got two daughters.' He said, 'I know. I seen them. One of them looks like you all over. Got a lot of her mother in her.' That's when I started thinking hey, I'm an auntie. Well, one day I met them. One of them, well, she was the spitting image of myself. She was a white girl, but that's my shadow, like a shadow reflected back onto me. She looked different, blonde hair and things like that, but there was a lot of me in her. I just couldn't help looking at her. Everywhere she went I followed her with my eyes. Knocked silly. Anthony say to me, 'Mum, she got a lot of you in her.' I said to him, 'She's my sister's daughter.' Everything just clicked. It just flowed out automatically. She went back to her mum. 'I found my Mum.' We ended up taking them down to Gnowangerup and all around there. I told them that's where your grandparents are, and Hilary. I took them down there to see where Hilary is buried. I see a lot of Hilary through her girls. That was beautiful, but I don't think it's settled in their minds yet. They just had a different life to us.

10

Travel, work and a new life

I LET THE dust settle after Hilary died, but not long after I knew I had to do something for my own life. So, bugger this. I'm going. I went and said goodbye to my little sister, told her, 'You're with Mum and Dad now.'

I went right around Australia, hitchhiking. I had some fun in my teenage years. Never worried about no one. The sixties was good. I had a good life. Real good time. I thought it was good times. Whoever was staying with me didn't, but I did have fun. We were a hippie mob – walk around with those big sloppy clothes on. But they were beautiful. Go to Cottesloe and I sit with all the wadjalas. They reckon, 'Come this way, you Noongar.' See you, I got friends. Back in the sixties I went everywhere. Just get a ride from one town to the other. Get a ride on them big trucks or maybe someone will come and say, 'Auntie, we're going to Darwin. You coming?' My Auntie May Garlett said to me, 'I'm going to Darwin. Sold my old man's house.' I looked at her. 'Come along with me, girl,' she said. 'Be my company.'

And that's what I done, went to Darwin, from Perth. No worries. I stayed in Darwin for about six months. I had a ball! It was lovely. Real good time. I needed that. Lived in the caravan with Auntie May, but not for long. I went to the Prep Hotel, had a room there. No money coming to get me, only dole and I not going to be on that. That's when I got that job. These white people were learning me to be a barmaid. I turned out to be a pretty good one, too. Got on with everyone, black, white, brindled, yellow and all. Prep Hotel had black and white sides. Blacks wasn't allowed to go into the white area and the whites wasn't allowed to go over with the blacks. But I never worried about that. My job was on the black side, but sometimes I'd go and work over in the white side. Nobody never said nothing. And those beautiful stockmen in those beautiful clothes with their boots and spurs. They was so handsome! Tall, dark and handsome.

And Auntie May sold the caravan and she said, 'I'm catching an aeroplane back.' She wanted me to have some money but I had enough money of my own. My Auntie wanted me to get a ride with her on that aeroplane back to Perth. I said to her, 'I love you Auntie, but I hate aeroplanes. Just look at them!' You wouldn't catch me on an aeroplane. Who's going to fall out of an aeroplane up there? This ground's too hard! Look at all them rocks and things! Nah, you wouldn't catch me in one. It's worse than when we flying along in the car and I'm lying on the floor. Anthony, my son, he couldn't help laughing. 'Get up Mum, what you lying on the floor for? I'll slow down.' I said I remember accidents from my Mum and Dad, so I said no. It hurts little bit thinking about that. I *hate* speed. So he slowed down. So, I told my Auntie I like to see the scenery and I'm going to keep going right around, working here, there and everywhere. Get a job here. As long as I had money. I always had money. And travel I did, on my own. I was gone two or three years. Not a care in the world. It was lovely. I really enjoyed it. By the time I come back, I was ready for home then and start my new life.

I missed out on my brother's wedding and the Quairading mob was all upset over that. So I said oh no, couldn't make it. But I caught up with it, explained that it was the rainy season up there and I couldn't have come home anyway. It was impossible; all the roads was blocked by water. After I explained why I couldn't make it, it was okay after that. See this little tiny woman. Shook her little hands. Realised that's my sister-in-law. Now she's as big as a house. Bigger than me! They were in Katanning.

I enjoyed my life. Worked my way around Australia. I always had a job, everywhere I went. The first year was a bit frightening, but I sort of got used to travelling, hitchhiking around, getting a ride from town to town. That was a good life. I could say I've been there and done that. I had a good mate. Her and her boyfriend looked after me. Hippies.

Come and go any time you feel like it. There used to be a mob of idiots all sitting in a park like this, all around in a big circle, singing and carrying on. You were one of the family. And that was a good time to grow up in, in the sixties. Everybody knew what they wanted.

After Darwin I went to Cairns, up in Queensland. And that was a joyride. Riding around with all these happy people. You had to be happy, you high. Cloud 9 up here. Yeah, I been there, done it. Pot was the main actor. Just starting to find out what it was all about. In the sixties it was fun years, eh? I was being young and stupid, but I never played up. It was just good fun. Best years of our lives. And you done what you wanted to do. And you enjoyed doing it. They were good times. I grew up in the best years, I think. They were fantastic. Freedom from everything for the first time. Peace. I had lots of friends, Noongars and wadjalas. And my gang used to get wild with me, tell me, 'You Noongar, you not wadjala.' Never used to worry about it. No, I got my mates. And then the 70s sort of slowing down, but we was still having a good time.

No worries for a while. I lived in Perth. Watching all the idiots. Got sick of it. I never even got into jail. In the lockup once when I was about 26 years old, because I was with the wrong people at the wrong time who shouldn't be on those premises in East Perth there. We was at a vacant block, that's all. Police come and we all got thrown in the rat van. Frightened me. Oh, funny fellas, the police. They reckon, 'You be the first one in the bus directly. You watch, you going to Bandyup now.' And that was frightening. I said, 'Where this Bandyup?' Don't even know where Bandyup is. I told them I never been to jail. Police, they rang the prison up, Bandyup, if they know of Helen Nellie. They say there's no record of her here. I think I was lucky there because I got frightened of jail. They let us out in the afternoon. I weren't drunk. I used to hate the stuff – and the smoking. And for years after I never even touch a drink. Went to court. They said you know what you better do? We're going to give you a bus fare back to Gnowangerup. You get on that bus this afternoon and we don't want to see you again. Give me a free ride. That John K. Watts, that big cheeky old sergeant, whatever he was. I was glad to get away from him. He used to be a big sergeant. And the Noongars, he'd talk to us like talking to a Noongar. You knew where he was coming from. And all the other girls, half of them did six months, twelve months in jail.

Before that I was working around Perth and after that, I went home to Gnowangerup then I went to Moora and Geraldton for a while. Got used to my family there. Then back to Albany. Settled down, down there. Sick of running around. Still enjoyed life. They were the good days. Them days I wouldn't want to be anywhere else.

≈

While I was in Albany, I stayed with my dear old sister them days, my first cousin Rita. And we found out that my Uncle had died. And I said to my other cousin, Gwenny, 'We have to go to his funeral.' And we had no rides. Everybody was too full. Just couldn't get a ride that day so we got on the road. We got to Gnowangerup, buried my dear old Uncle Malcolm, my mother's brother, the one who taught me how live to be a Noongar. Had my tears. That's another thing; I thought I was going to have Uncle Malcolm forever. I would have took care of Uncle Malcolm and Auntie Bonnie if I was a bit sensible.

Walking back, hitchhiking from Gnowangerup to Albany, all of a sudden I went numb all over. I said to my Gwenny, 'Hey sister, help me out.' She said, 'You all right? You look pale.' I said, 'Find the biggest stick you can find and hit me. Big stick.' And she looked at me as if I was stupid, mad. 'Yeah,' I said, 'biggest stick, hardest one. See one of them mungart trees? (They're hard wood, they're like sandal-wood. It won't break at all.) Get that and whack me with it.' 'No', she said. 'No way, Helen. I don't do things like that. You my sister, for goodness sake. You going off your head!' Well, maybe I was. I said, 'No, girl, just hit me hard, please. I'm either dying or I got something wrong with me. Just hit me somewhere, please!' Standing up talking to her just like I'm going to fall over and die. I was so numb I thought I might be dead already. So she cracked me with this big stick. 'You felt that?' she said. 'I'm sorry, sis, I'm sorry.' And I'm saying, 'Crack me anywhere! In the head, or on the knees, anywhere you feel like doing it. Do it again!' 'No! I might knock you out.' Poor Gwenny, she was shaking; she couldn't even talk to me. 'You my sister, I don't want to do this to you!' I said, 'Just hit me as hard as you can with that stick.' And then she done it again. Bang! Across the back with this big, hard stick. 'That hurt?' I told her I never felt nothing. She was the weakest hit out. She looked at me and said, 'I'm not doing that again, sister.' Oh, every time I think of it I could cry laughing.

She used to be a fast runner. She just run along the road. I'm singing out that I'm going to die. And she come running back, 'No, don't you die.' I said, 'Hit me again!' But no, she wouldn't do it. I said, 'There's an electric fence there. I wonder if it'll kill me.' She reckon, 'No! I'll fight you right here if you try to run into that.' So, I told her I can manage until we get back to Albany. We was hitchhiking. Anyway, these people come along that knew me. White people. They said, 'Jump in, Helen.' The driver, him and his wife, he looked at me; he was worried I wasn't all right and he said I need to go straight and see my doctor. So they drove me to the terrace to see my doctor. Them and Gwenny said, 'You going straight in to Dr Inchley.'

Old Dr Inchley, he was a real understanding old doctor. That's our doctor. I went in to see him. I must have been about 22, 23 then. He said, 'You know, Helen, you know of anyone in your family with sugar?' I said, 'I remember Dad giving himself needles. What's that for?' I say to my doctor, and he reckon, 'Well, he had sugar.' He had a little bottle about two inches long. He used to needle himself and chase us if we didn't behave ourselves – show us that needle. Anyway, he told me, 'You got sugar.' I said, 'How come I got that?' He said that sugar runs natural in any family and usually the eldest one or second eldest gets the father's sickness. He reckons it's nothing to be frightened of. 'You just got to live with it. It can be good. It can be bad, but you got to fight it.' The first time I ever found out, same as my Dad. Just found out when I was about 22. I ended up with sugar, but I didn't have to have needles. Mum was good. She never had no sickness, not that I can remember. She was always healthy. Yeah, Dad was a diabetic and my brother got that, and so did I. That really got me down.

I was still feeling numb all over. He examined me, him and his nurse and they told Gwen that I had to go straight into hospital. 'I got to put you in hospital,' he said, 'because there's something else coming up. I need to operate.' I said, 'What, sugar?' 'No, but it might have something to do with sugar.' He told Gwenny, 'She's got something wrong with her very bad and if she don't go in, well, we might lose her.' That frightened me. 'Yeah, but we got no money for taxis.' 'I'll pay for the taxi,' he said, 'and there'll be a bed waiting for you in the Albany Regional Hospital when you get there.' When I went there, sure enough, they put me on a wheelchair. Gwen come along crying and I had a bit of tear myself. I said, 'Don't make me nervous, sister, I feel frightened enough.' Put me in hospital for nearly two weeks to check me out before they operated.

Well, I was pleased I went into hospital. It was gallstones. They reckoned they were about as big as a pea and they had to operate on me, remove them gallstones. They can kill you. Him and Dr Lynch done that operation on me. Biggest operation I had. I thought I was going to die. I was all tied up with all these wires all over me. I couldn't seem to move, all these wires and that bag hanging on my side. I didn't want to see nobody, but all people come to see me and I said, 'I'm not moving. I'm staying here until I get well enough to go.' I think with me I'm a very strong-minded person. No one telling me no.

And there was this white lady. She come and sat by my bed and she said to me, 'You know what?' as she combing my hair. 'They won't let me see my twins.' They let her see them first for a little while but they took them away and later they said to her that her babies had died, two of them. And that sort of hit something in her head. She screamed that hospital down. I could hear her coming and I can't move. Ah, don't. When she come past all the old people in the passage, punched an old lady up and down; old man, pushed him over. Ah, no. The nurse came to me and she said, 'Did she come in here yet?' I said, 'No.' They said they waiting here in my room for her.

She walked in nicely. The nurses and the doctors was standing there waiting for her. She come, combing my hair. Combing it nice. They put that needle into her to ease her down, and she just sat talking to me. I talking to her. I say,

'They gone, they gone to heaven. They were little angels, they were meant to be little angels.' 'Oh,' she said, 'I never looked at life that way.' I said, 'They still with you. Might be a memory, but they'll always be flying around you. They know. The Lord, Jesus, got them.' She said, 'Thank you.' And the preacher was there and I told him, 'I talking about they not dead, they just little angels flying around her.' And he said, 'You know what? You a very thoughtful lady. Look where you are.' I said, 'Well, I didn't want her to bash me! A couple of old womans got it up there.' He couldn't help laughing. He said, 'That's the best I heard all day. You made my day, anyway.' He brought me an apple back next day. Big, red apple. The sister come, she reckon, 'Whatever you said to her it sort of worked. She quietened right down now.' Well I felt good. I laid back and went to sleep.

Dr Lubich – if there was a stubborn doctor, it was Dr Lubich. He was one of the specialists for Noongar people. He knew everybody from the reserve and every Noongar woman's sickness. You can't seem to get away from him, old Lubich. He was the devil man, wish you'd never met him. But he was solid. And he'd tell us straight out, 'You Noongars are stupid. Look after yourselves. Some of you are beautiful ladies. You know, get yourselves together.' Real nasty, that's how he used to talk to us; he was solid in his way of telling us. Oh, we didn't like it, but we loved it. If they said, 'You got to go and see Dr Lubich today,' we say, 'We not going there. We going to see Dr Inchley. But sometimes I had to see Dr Lubich and I used to come back and tell Dr Inchley what he's like. 'Don't worry about him. He's old and childish,' he said, 'but he's a good specialist. He's the one who operated on you to save your life.' 'Oh, thank you for putting it that way, doctor.'

Dr Inchley had cancer, but I didn't know that at the time. He saved my life, but couldn't save his own. And I treasure those memories. I thanked him from the bottom of my heart. When I found out he died, I was in Perth. I went to Albany where his house was and I said I'm very sorry to his wife, family. 'Thank you, you the first Noongar lady that done that in all our days here in Albany.' I knew I had a friend there. He saved my life. So anyway, I sort of come out of the hospital after being in there for nearly two months – had all my belly things hanging out here. They cleaned all that out. Had a good rest. I was able to go home. I had to go back to the Albany Reserve.

Then, things was changing again. My old people started fading away and leaving us. It felt real empty in Gnowangerup. For a lot of us we always had someone we could go and yarn with. What better people than the old fellas.

11

Harry John

AFTER I GOT back from my travels around Australia, I stayed on the Albany reserve with my cousin. Then, I got that job in Albany, Tom the Cheap Grocer. The mayor of Albany got it for me. Old Mary Thompson, her name was. She was a little old lady. She loved Noongar people. I knew her from the reserve. She used to do everything for Noongars. Them days there was no Noongar girls looking for a job, in the sixties going well on into the seventies. Well I wanted a job, just to get away from the reserves. 'Bring her into the office today,' she said to Auntie Ida and Auntie Lila, that's my two old aunties, my Dad's people. And they brought me in there and she was sitting in her office. 'Oh, this is Helen?' 'Yes, that's our niece and she looking for that job.' Anyway the boss from Tom the Cheap Grocer came over. 'This is Helen,' said Mary Thompson. 'At the moment she's up at the reserve living with her sister.' And the boss said, 'We'd better find a place for her. Anyway, the boss talked to someone and then said, 'Well, we'll hire her on Monday if she's available.' I jumped at it.

So they bought me new clothes, twin set, skirt, stockings, new shoes, oh I really look like a wadjala. Old Mary Thompson, she thought it was great, dressing me up. And all the girls looking. 'Look at her, thinks she's great.' I tell them, 'I got a job, I'm going to my first shop job and I'm the only Noongar in Albany got a job in the shop, so shush.'

I was enjoying my work that much. Every time parcels or this thing would fall to the ground or break I used to pack them all up because we weren't allowed to sell them. Write on the new one the cost, pack 'em all in the shelves, wash all the shelves down after and make sure the shelves was neat. I was good at that. I had a lot of training for that in the Mission. That was good.

Well, anyway, I'm working and I was racing this girl to the toilet every half hour. That's funny. So, Mary Thompson was concerned about me being sick. She was like an old mother and she said, 'I think I'd better take you two to Dr Inchley.' Me and this other white girl. She was solid, my mate. We're standing there so innocent at Dr Inchley's. 'Now you girls are very naughty girls.' 'How come? We got a job.' 'Got jobs all right. But you don't know where you coming from,' he said. 'You're three months pregnant, the pair of you.' Well my world just shattered. I'm having a baby! Out of wedlock. It was frightening. No Mission left to go run and hide in.

My baby's father, he was a big blackfella, very handsome, well dressed, a real gentleman when he was sober. Everyone used to call him Charlie Pride because he looked like Charlie Pride. We met in Gnowangerup. We was together three or four years, on and off. But he was just like a sleeping mate – them days in Albany was very cold. I never been that sort of person to change partners. But he was a terrible drinker. When he was drinking, he was a wicked man. He was that cruel, jealous, very jealous. He was terrible. Violent. You can't talk to him. He was the type of bloke who'd just say, 'Where she is? Is she here?' His sisters, they protected me from him. 'No,' they'd say, 'She not here.' I be standing back, hiding. I had to get away from him. He started being a real standover and I wasn't used to that life. If he wasn't trying to cut my hair he'd be chasing me with something. He did cut my hair. I was pretty and had beautiful long hair. He reckon if I had short hair I wouldn't be pretty and no fellas would want me. I warned him I was going to leave him, but he just say, 'You won't leave, you won't leave.' But I had my own mind and I did leave. He knew I was pregnant, but I didn't want him in it.

So, when I found out I was pregnant I went to my friends, Mum and Pop Dasborough in Albany for a while. I used to call him Dad. He rang up all around and talked to my friend, Miss Blunt at the Gnowangerup Bible Institute. I used to know her since I was little girl, ten or eleven. She sort of took me under her wings like a big sister. And I never had that. Anyway, she took me everywhere. She said, 'You know what? There might be place going in Mogumber Mission.' I said, 'What that is?' 'It's a Methodist Mission. They take ladies in when you're pregnant. We're going to leave you there, decide whether you going to keep the baby or have him fostered out.' Well, it took a long time for me to think about that. But I thinking I really don't know about rearing a baby. I knew a lot about kids, but I was at a silly age where you just want to go out and have fun. I'm sorry I done that because in the long run, it hurt. But it happened. My cousin was there, Cedric Jacobs and his wife Margaret – she was a white girl. And Cedric Jacobs, he said, 'Yeah, I know Helen, that's my little sister. Bring her up here.'

And they took me to Mogumber Mission. Mogumber was a horrible Mission. The looks of it was spooky. It was very old. It was running long before the forties. The mystery of the trees, they can talk to you at times, even when you walk through on your own. Eww, you get an awful, creepy feeling. My cousin Cedric back then he was a preacher and I used to stay with him and Margaret. Everything was there, open for me. And I never ever got over that. It's just like the doors from heaven is opening up to me. Someone must be looking after me so I'm going to do my best.

They didn't have a hospital at Mogumber, but we was able to go to Bennett House in Perth where mothers can go and stay there till they have their baby. And when I was at Bennett House I used to go out with the boys and girls, moonlighting, just go and check on the old graves at the East

Perth cemetery, that's how stupid we was. Three of us, big girls, boodjari ones, pregnant. I used to outrun them other two. Other one was too fat, other one was two skinny, but she was frightened, because she wasn't from that country, she was from way up north. The other girls thought they would leave us, but I left them for dust. Running back they reckon, 'We going to tell sister on you because you not allowed to run.' I used to run across the park and everybody, Noongars, used to say, 'Slow down, boodjari one. We're going to tell that mob at Bennett House on you.' I think that's why Harry must have been so tough. I used to run everywhere, beat them girls at everything. They'd sit down on the side of the road, 'We going to tell on you. You not supposed to be running.' But I used to sleep. I used to feel it in my sleep. Once you got to know everybody that wasn't such a bad Mission, but I still think Gnowangerup was boss.

I stayed for nearly four months in Bennett House before I went in to have the baby in King Edward Memorial Hospital. I had a cousin I never seen for years – another old sister. And we was always walking past each other in the passageway at Bennett House. Other old aunties they think they all knew but they wasn't too sure. And then Auntie Bonnie said to me, 'You know this woman here?' 'No, who?' She said to this woman, 'You know this one here?' 'No,' she said. 'Who she is?' 'You know that's your own sister there. You Nellies.' 'What?' she shouted. 'What?' I shouted on this other side. 'You two blood! You sisters. Your two fathers are brothers.'

Well, she nearly fainted. And I thinking how I'm going to bend over to rub this woman if she faints. Oh, Auntie Bonnie, help me please. If she faints, help me. She said, 'How you know she's going to do that?' I said. 'It must be sister's intuition.' Auntie Bonnie said, 'You two my nieces!' So anyway, she cried and I cried and Auntie Bonnie, Auntie Rosie, them all cried for us. Fancy, two Nellies. She was my elder sister, Iris Nellie. Colley, they used to call her. She reckons I look a lot like Lydia. I was frightened of her; they reckon she kaat wara, gone in the head. And she's standing right in front of me, mental case woman. I couldn't do nothing because my tummy's too big. I couldn't hardly sit down, let alone run. Well, she looked after me, really supportive. She really became the boss there. She said, 'My little sister, she's having a baby.'

I never got pregnant until I'm older. I would have had three kids. All Smiths. They were Noongars from my son's father, Bill Smith. Two boys and a girl. But I couldn't carry the other two right through. I was lucky to carry Harry John, my son, through. He was my third pregnancy. That was a mistake, but it was lovely. But I was thankful for that little part of the bible.

Had the baby on 28 March 1978. I was 30 years old. I named him Harry John Nellie, no Smith in it. He kept the Smith looks, but that's all. He's a Nellie, old George Nellie's oldest grandson. I was still very young. He was born in King Edward Memorial Hospital in Subiaco. Anyway I'm lying back in my bed and I look and this big dark bloke walking past. I felt terrible. Couldn't be Bill Smith! I hope it's not him. But it was my cousin-in-law, my brother-in-law. 'Hey,' I said, 'I thought you was a big African man,' because he was dark as anything and a big bloke. Norman Rowe his name is. He laughed and he say, 'What you in here for? Lorraine down there and you upstairs; she had a little girl. I come up to see Lorraine. Come down with me, we'll go down have a look at her.' I told him I had a boy. 'Come and have a look at him, who you think he look like.' 'Ah,' he reckon, 'that's a Smith all over there. That's Bill's.' I said, 'Yeah, that's my boy.' Pretty-looking boy. He's lying back crying. I look at him, picked him up, nursed him. But there was just a barrier there. I didn't know whether they were going to take Harry off me then, or later on. I was almost scared to love him.

So, I had to go back to Mogumber Mission, straight from King Edward, but only for a little while, about a week. I said to Mr Clarke, the Superintendent at Mogumber, old Matty Clarke, 'I'd like to foster Harry John for a little while until I find myself again.' 'That's a good idea,' he said. 'Not really, that's my baby.' I was mixed up and needed him to be fostered because I was only a young person and I like to be going places. I was a bit too young to have children. I didn't want to be tied down. I want to get up and be myself for a while, go out and work. I needed that freedom. I know I was selfish. There was places available for little boys and girls to be fostered.

Harry John had to stay at Mogumber until someone could foster him. He was already being bottle-fed. I didn't have much milk anyway. I tell you, I was frightened when I had Harry after I finished feeding him because I remember what happened to my cousin back in Borden. They reckon, 'Don't walk around here like you are. Snake, any old snake, he'll follow you for your tits.' This time they'll all smell for that baby milk. That's an old Noongar's tale there from way back. My old Auntie Ellie used to tell me all that, because she was like an old witchdoctor; she was a powerful old lady. I used to call her Old Mummy.

And Harry John, they already had a Dutch couple in touch with them, so he was booked. They was making arrangements to take him from Mogumber. I never met them, but I knew Harry John was going to a good home. I knew in my heart that I'll come back and pick him up. Anyway, went back to Bennett House, but just for a couple of days. They showed me how to draw milk into a bottle with a pump. So, I went back to Albany. That's what I done – what the Welfare wanted. That was the biggest mistake I made in life.

I had already left this awful man. I got a job in the woollen mills, but I drifted around a lot. Went to Geraldton and to Moora – sightseeing. The old people told me in Perth that I had a lot of family up north. I wanted to get up there and meet them all and find out who's who and what's what. Get to know family. And brother, I'm glad I done that. I know where I am now. Best part of my life.

Then I got a lift to Wilmington in South Australia. Stayed there for about four months. I enjoyed that, earning some money. It was a lovely town. Everybody was like they knew everybody. Come in, you welcome. Wilmington had no prejudices. Blacks and wadjalas all treated the same. Shearers mainly all there and big farms. It was solid.

They had the shearer's quarters on one side and we was in with the girls. All the girls used to sweep all the wool off the tables, sort things. I used to do it sometimes. Hands used to be so terrible after. But it was good. I enjoyed that. You knew what you doing and knew how much money you going to get. I knew a little bit about money by then.

They said I got to learn to cook. Got a job as a cook's assistant. The cook, he was the lowest cook I ever had the time to be with. He was a drunken, dribbling old man, but didn't he used to cook beautiful food! In the end, they put a thing around his face to stop him dribbling in the food and a big hat on him. Tubby old clown. I forget his name, Toby or Taylor, but he was a clown. Slim Dusty sings about the shearer's cook and how low down they can be. Well, this was one of them. 'Now, come here girl, I'll soon show you how to cook.' Well, this old man teach me. Rough and ready stuff. Slap everything in. They don't know what they eating. Put a kangaroo tail in it or a bobtail in, fill it up with fresh meat. I used to know what he's cooking and I thinking, you are a very sneaky old cook. Real bushman cook. Those boys come in from shearing and they say, 'Ooo, this is beautiful!'

They love it! And they look at me pulling a face and they go, 'Why you go like that?' I thought, 'If you knew what I knew, but you'll find out one day.' And he's looking straight at me, too, the old cook. I used to stick my head up and walk away. He used to wipe his nose up his arm. I say to him, 'What you doing that for?' 'Ah, shut up, girl, anything to put a bit of flavour in – they don't know.' I said, 'You don't do that with me!' And he reckon, 'You the first black woman who ever told me that.' I said, 'Well, you got no choice here, I'm from the West. We been brought up in missions. We know what cleanliness is. Sooner they sack you, the better.' I said I want to go back to Albany, but he say, 'You can go back to West Australia. We don't need you here. But you earn the money before you go. You not getting away from me that easy.' He was a boss old man.

After a while, I was homesick and went back to Albany. Got to Adelaide, jumped on a train. I was in my thirties and I was glad to get home. That's when I really started to connect with my family, the Williamses. My little nieces and nephews was growing up and they was skipping school. I told them they had to go to school. They looked up to me, called me Mother Goose too.

12

Kalgoorlie

SINCE UNCLE MALCOLM died, I was getting a bit lost. Well, my friend, an old missionary, she used to be in Gnowangerup Mission – old Miss Allen, she said to me I can't stay in Albany because I still wasn't completely better. She come up and she said to me, 'Miss Blunt wants you in the Bible Institute in Gnowangerup until you get on your feet.' I said, 'Well, there's a blessing. I wouldn't be able to do anything down here in Albany except torment my poor old sister.' So there must have been something with me down through the years, you know, to happen that way. And I thinking someone must be taking care of me, looking after me. I was set on finding out about myself instead of following all the drunks around. So I said, 'Yeah, I'll go.' Couldn't hardly walk.

I was that thankful when I went up to Gnowangerup. Mr Millen, Superintendent then of the Gnowangerup Bible Institute, he took me to the Institute. He knew us all since we was in the Mission. The institute is a bible school for young Noongar people who wants to go to college and that wasn't far across the road from where the old Mission was, in Gnowangerup. Beautiful place. Miss Blunt was there and all the students, must have been about six or eight of them. I knew most of them from the Mission. And she showed me my room, bed and all, right next to her room. She said, 'You just rest here till you find your strength and we'll look for somewhere you can go to work.' I just went off to sleep. Couple of days later I was able to cook for the students.

Well, after that I sort of picked my strength up. The hardest part was losing Mum and Dad. If I can go through that, that's the biggest test in my life. There must be something good around the corner for me. So that's how I learnt how to be me. Grew up with a lot of people telling me what I should do and what I shouldn't do. But I was stubborn enough to say, 'No, I'm making my own decisions. It's my life, not yours. I like my way just the way I am.'

But then, Miss Allen spoke to the Dasboroughs and asked them if I could stay with them. Oh, that was just wonderful. I stayed with Pop and Mrs Dasborough for a year, maybe two years. Did odd jobs around Albany and worked as a nurse's aide at an old people's home, Seaton Lodge.

Then Miss Blunt found me a job in Kurrawang Mission. She said, 'You know what? There's a Mission out in Kalgoorlie.' I didn't think there was any there. Cundeelee was the only one, we always talk about how they getting on and how we getting on. 'Oh no,' she said, 'this one is only seven miles out of Kalgoorlie.' It was a little Mission about twelve kilometres out of Kalgoorlie, only about three miles off the road. She said, 'There's a place open there.' I told her, 'I never been to that country, it's not my country; I come from the Stirling Ranges.' 'They want someone to help them look after boys.' Boys' hostel. They said to me, 'You're used to it. You've been to the Mission. Same as that.' And I said, 'Yeah, I'll jump to that.' That's when I first went to the goldfields.

So, I come up from Albany to Kurrawang Mission. The bus pulled up at the gate. I told the bus driver I never been there before. I was that frightened. He turned around and asked all the other passengers if they knew that Mission, but nobody did. And he went back and asked the other passengers if they'd like to go into Kurrawang, because she don't know anyone. The people said, 'We'd love to.' I thinking ah, they're solid. I thanked him, shook his hand and I said, 'All right if I could sit on the step, that step to go up and down near the driver?' 'Yes,' he said. So, he turned that bus into that long driveway and took that bus right to the door. It was only three miles, but it felt like it's a long way into the Kurrawang Mission. Well, I sat there looking and all of a sudden, I can see a lot of Wongis standing round the bus, looking. Everybody all wondering what they got big bus coming in here for. I was shamed when I jumped out the bus, grabbed my case, coat. When I look, the first face I seen was this wonderful old Wongi man. I knew him, he was my old Uncle, old Jack Ridley. He looking at me and he knew me straight away. 'Ah,' he said, 'I waiting for you.' I was that pleased I knew somebody there. Him and his wife, Melva and little kids there, my sisters and brothers. Only one dear old face I knew and I sort of settled right down there. He was related to my Dad! These little kids was all little dolls, little black dolls. He reckon, 'Family, my family.' That's how I was accepted in Wongi, first time in my life. He was the first real dark Wongi I knew. And he reckon, 'I know your father, he my family.' If your father come from there, that's your country. That's where you come from. They were beautiful people to me, you know, I had a feeling that I had a family.

That was a lot of learning too, but I was looked after at the Mission – taught a lot of things. Going to a place where you don't know no one and you don't know who to talk to, that old one he told all of Kalgoorlie that his niece come from Albany, southwest and she's at Kurrawang with us. And that felt so good. Worked in the laundry there. Taught other girls who had just come in from the desert. Called me Mumma Loo. Some times I had about sixty kids, little boys. Wash and comb their hair, make sure they're clean and dressed for school, make all their beds and make sure tea was ready for them when they come home. That was good. I enjoyed that. It was like in the Mission again. We even went to church.

So, I used to help them with cooking now and then and washing kid's sheets and pillowcases and towels. That was a good job. I really enjoyed that. Fold them all up when they're clean, bring them all in. Sometimes there was fifty kids, sometimes there was a hundred kids, all come in from different missions like Cundeelee, Leonora, Mount Margaret up north way in the desert. Little kids from all over the place. Anyway, I used to have fun with them all. Lots of Noongar kids from down south. Kids I used to know. And they all knew me. Used to introduce them all round to everybody. It was good. Yeah, that was good. And girls I used to know in Esperance through my brother, when he used to be in the Peddler's Hostel for boys there, they all working, mainly farm work, they all knew me from there. 'That's Russell Nellie's sister,' they'd say.

I was taught all little things by the Wongi mob. Sit down when old men and old woman talking, they'd tell me a lot of things. That's why I tell Noongars that I been brought up by legends. Wongi could talk with their chin, lip, when they don't feel like talking. They sitting in the bush. I thinking what they going like that for, lip wobbling and chin jutting out and in real quick. Old Popeye Johnson, he say to me, 'You, you Noongar girl. Them fellas sitting in the bush, they want you to go there.' And I thought they was pulling a face at me. I took off this other way, to Kurrawang. After that I just used to kill myself laughing over that, too.

So I followed these little boys, must have been ten of them, eleven of them, from time to time. Little kids used to show me all this bush thing up there. And they reckon if you eat that you won't go thirsty. They got little fruits and inside are fresh growing things that could grow into a tree, but you pick them this time now when it's raining; ah, it's the sweetest bush tucker I ever tasted. Or you could warm them up on the side of the coal fire and ah, it's a beautiful taste, like cooking carrots on the side of the fire. Lovely and sweet like carrots.

One time I was just walking the little kids through the bush. We was going back to the Mission and I was singing along with them and all of a sudden I looked. This old man stood in the front of me. Don't know where he come from. He said, 'You right. You girl. You nuari one. You from south-west?' I said, 'Yeah.' 'See that road there? You walk back to Kurrawang. Don't look back. You not allowed this way.' So I was thinking I wonder what that was. I said, 'Why?' 'That's all man way there. You go back. These kids'll take you back. You a stranger here.' But he was laughing telling me.

Then I turned around and when I looked for that old man, can't see him. I telling this old lady at the Mission who was helping me look after the boys. I said, 'This old man came out of nowhere, like he fell out of a tree, frightened me.' 'No,' she said, 'that's Lore way, that way there. You're not allowed to go there. But you'll learn it from time to time.' Blackfellas up there, that's their way of life. Lore men. I think he was a lookout, keeping people away from the sacred ground. Like old boss man. You listen to him and you do what he tell you, you'll never go wrong. My good old

Uncle there, Uncle Jack Ridley, he's from Wongi, he was a Lore man. I didn't know that at the time. I was pleased I had somebody up there I could talk to. He used to tell me, 'You can't go too far over there, my girl.' 'Why?' 'That's all man country. That's Lore way. No woman's allowed there. These kids will tell you. They'll tell you where can go and where you can't. They'll learn you, they'll teach you,' he said. And they're like that, Wongis. And I learnt all the secrets of the bush, all the places where womans can't go. Later, I was telling Popeye Johnson about this man coming from nowhere. 'Ah, you Noongar, what you walking through the bush that way for? Never mind, you my girl.'

Another thing I learnt that never lie outside on the hot nights. And I used to say, 'Why? Why do I can't lie outside? Because sometimes I like to put my rug down and go to sleep.' 'You want to be charmed by these old mans? That's their way of life here. They grab young girls, take them to be their wives. But you might be all right, see you're a stranger up here. You Noongar.' But they was charmed with me because my hair was way down to my waist. I had peroxide in it and I used to wear it up top in one big lump or let it flow. Well, it must have looked a fire to these old people. Never seen a black woman with hair like that. 'Nuari one.'

And the Wongis, I thinking they was swearing at me. Nuari, that means nice looking, but I didn't know that. I thought they was swearing at me. I run, left a wheelbarrow there full of food. Run all the way home. They was going to chase me back to the boys' dormitory there. I'm yelling, 'Auntie Gladys, Auntie Gladys!' She said, 'What's going on, Helen? Where the tea? We got to start cooking now. Kids will be home soon.' I told her, 'Wheelbarrow way up there, at the shop. I want to go home on the next bus to Albany.' She laughed her head off. 'Don't tell me they was swearing at you again.' 'Yes, they was swearing at me.' 'Oh,' she said. 'That's no good.' Anyway, she walked back up and got the wheelbarrow. She say to those fellas, 'What you saying to her?' 'Aah, nuari, nuari, nuari girl. She from southwest. That was nice-looking lady, nice-looking woman. And she got lovely hair. We never seen hair like that,' they reckon. 'You not allowed to think like that. She's a Noongar girl.' The oldies used to laugh. 'Nah, nuari.'

Well, I wouldn't come out of that place. I just locked myself behind the door after I finished work. 'Come out, Helen, it's hot.' I'll say, 'No, you right. I'll talk to them through the window.' And the boys used to sing out, 'Auntie Helen, come and play cricket with us.' 'No, you right.' And old Pop Ridley come there, him and his wife and he said, 'Come on, you Noongar. I'll look after you; you our niece. Your father is my cousin.' He said, 'I won't let them talk to you like that.' No, they swearing at me, Uncle. He killed himself laughing. Anyway, I got outside, peeping around, looking to see if I could see any old Wongi around so I could run and lock myself up again. Oh, it took me a year, but after a while I sort of got used to it. I was there at Kurrawang for two years I think.

And young men are sent off to find a wife. Dad, he was Wongi. They sent Dad off to find a woman and he found Mum. Even now, old people tell them, 'Go down south. Find yourself a woman. Start your own family. We don't want you up here. Come back and see us sometime.' They do that to a lot of Wongis I noticed. Tell them, 'Go long, this not your home any more. You young man.' Lot of boys I see went through missions like that told to get out and go.

Wongi mob, they know my Dad, or they know of him, who he was. Wongi say, 'This your home, always remember. You family.' And that was the loveliest feeling out. I felt really at home there. It took me years to understand what they said. And they say, 'You learn Wongi, eh?' I said, 'Yowa.' That mean hello, I'm talking to you. Also mean yes. I know more Wongi than I do Noongar; learnt all the words. I learnt it when I went to Kal. They say, 'See, you one of us. You Wongi.' I said, 'I Noongar. I got my home down there.' They say, 'Yeah, you might have been brought up there, but we your family.'

So anyway, it was time for me to move. Is there any other jobs around Kalgoorlie? I said I had a lifetime of looking after little kids. These little boys will know who I am. Anyway, they said there's a vacancy at Nindee Hostel in Kalgoorlie, Boulder. I'll take that. They reckon it's in the laundry. Yeah, that's all right, it's still working with kids.

I love old Kal. If I had a chance, I'd go back up there any time. I got a lot of didjas and kurtas, that's sisters and brothers. I got to know all the Kalgoorlie mob. Wadjalas, Noongars. Noongar people down there too. Wongis, Yamatji. I knew everybody. Good fun with that lot, especially hangi days on the weekend. Every Sunday up in Kal. First the Wongi and Noongars make their way and Maoris on the other side. But the Maoris always boss. Ah, you could smell that meat cooking for miles. When they peel that bag, clean bags or banana leaves over and you could just go and pull your meat off and it'll melt in your mouth. Oh, how they do it. So beautiful. We used to all stand there with our plates. Have lemon or salt with it. The veggies and all, just right. Have a good beer. We all used to work them days. I had lots and lots of friends. Knew where they was all staying in Boulder and Kalgoorlie. Oh, that was the exciting times. Good mates. You mix in; didn't matter if you were black, white or brindle. That's made it all worthwhile for me. That was the best time of my life.

But some, they reckon, 'You like a widebella woman.' Widebella woman? I'm a Noongar. But they was meaning 'whitefella'. I said well, I'm proud of that. And that started me thinking. I thinking what am I doing things like this for. I'm a Noongar. I had to do everything spot on, like a white person. And Wongi reckon, 'Hey Helen, you white lady, widebella, widebella' in singing voice, stirring me up, but not nasty like. They could see it inside me, coming out.

No I'm not! I never used to worry about them. I'm here, I'm boss. Laugh at it. Then I stop and think that this brainwash must still have been in me for me to be like that. Time I start being a Noongar. I don't think I'd do that sort of way anymore. Never felt happy about it. Just who I am and they can take me as they see me. I'm comfortable with who I am and the best part of it, I found my tongue. I was the quietest person out; I used to hate people telling me what to do. I put my head down, don't talk, sit way in the back. And that was hard time and good times, and sit back now and laugh at it all. I been there and done it.

Anyway, that was where I met my first husband, in Kalgoorlie. I didn't like him at first. And he used to drive a big truck for Kleenheat Gas. And my family used to say to me, 'Huh! You know how to pick your man.' You know, have a joke with me. You could hear him for miles with all this thing all over, noise everywhere. And no, we don't like him, we don't like him. He's too noisy.

I run away. I come down to my brother's in Quairading. He come flying down after, begging for me to go back to marry him. So, old fools never learn. I went back. Put the ring on the finger. And that was it. Anyway that never lasted. We was married for not even six months and then I found something out about him. Not very nice. And it took the girls six months, nearly a year to tell me what was going on. That really upset me. These Wongi girls, they said, 'You don't come down we going to get you and see your husband, see where he is.' And there were all these night girls down there, up in Kal. Hay Street it was. It took, it seemed like a lifetime to get it into my head that he was actually doing that stuff in the front of me while I was sitting home washing clothes out, cleaning up and that – very good little wife for a while. Then, when it finally hit me that was it! I was glad to get rid of him and he was glad to get rid of me. That was the quickest wedding out.

After a long time in Kalgoorlie I used to tell them I'm going home, now, gotta go back Albany way. They reckon, no, you can't go – until I got my divorce. That time them old people come, ones I met and really cherished in life. They said you getting a divorce. When you get a divorce up here, it's like somebody die. That's our Lore. You got to go back to your own country for five years. I said I'll be glad to do that. I never waited, I was just up and out – gone. I had to do it because that was old Wongi way. You go back for five years to your country. So, I went home to Albany. That's why I never went back up there to Kal in a hurry.

Went back after five years and oh, I was like one of the family, 'cause I done the right thing. They was that welcoming, which only a Wongi can do. They're legend people. I'd go up tomorrow. I just like being there. I knew enough Wongi. I had a lot of friends who still teach me now a lot when we bump into each other. I'm not going to change from you fellas, you are like my families, my didjas. They all get pleased, too. 'Helen Nellie never change.' That's what they say, in singing voice. I loved it up there. I had friends, good mates, you know, go here, there and everywhere – enjoy life. And now it's different! You know, I got boys I used to look after in Kurrawang, Wongi way, now they Lore man. They went through the Lore, blackfella way. And they all beautiful boys. Anything I want, like, they give me, and I tell them nup, nup. Not allowed to say that. 'You Mumma Loo.' They all come back and say: 'We love you, Mum. Mumma Loo.' That means treasured Mum, love you Mum. That's what it means. 'You our Mum forever.'

And I still get it when I go back, Kalgoorlie, Leonora, Laverton; you know they all know who I am. 'Oh, we know you. You Mumma Loo, you look after us long time.' Now, older boys, they've all grown up and got childrens of their own. Tell them, 'That's your grandmother. She look after us when we little ones.' So, I got tons of grannies, Kalgoorlie, all right through. I'm proud of that.

And years later, one old lady come down and she put her head on my shoulder and she just cried her eyes out. 'Thank you for looking after my two boys. I was sick,' she said. 'You Mumma Loo. Yeah, you. That's your boys. Two mummies,' she said. 'Two Mumma Loos. You main one. Me, I'm there on the side.' They Lore men now. I tell her, 'You be proud of who you are.' Love 'em. All the little grannies you got. I come and kiss them like they my own children. Even now, they look at me, put their heads down, 'Big lady. Big lady.' Most of the boys now I seen them reared up in that Mission, seen them grow up to be young fellas, they all Lore men now, big bosses up there. 'Mumma Loo, you come up there, you welcome. Everything will be laid out for you.' And up there, you can't say no. Not allowed to say no. What they give you, yours. That's from their heart. Wongis tell me they're happy with what their decision is. Before, I didn't know about that, I used to tell them, 'Nah, nah. Money? Nah, don't need it. I got money.' Head down, they'd go away and cry. And I looking around at them other young girls and I say, 'What the –!?' 'Nah, you doing wrong thing, you say no. You get. What they give you, you take.' Now, old fellas come to me with money. I say, 'What that for?' But now I open my bag and put the money in there. Things like that, you know. 'Thank you for what you done for us. You enjoy.' And that's beautiful. Even now when I go back people come up give me a hundred dollars, three hundred dollars, all around up there. Oh, they're wonderful. 'You family.' They look at me and they say, 'You family, you Nellie.'

Old Popeye Johnson. He was a Lore man; a good Lore man. He was a Christian as well. He gave up being a Christian for a little while. For a while there was a few of them like that, but along the way it might have got too hard for them and they went back to the old ways. They all dead and gone now. But they were my family who made me welcome in Kalgoorlie. Old Popeye, he was a legend – a man, and a legend of his time. Big old fat fella. He was a real dark man, a happy-go-lucky fella and he had the most gorgeous smile.

I can see it now. He was such a funny old fella, couldn't help loving him. Everybody knew him, even tourists and that. He used to sit in the middle of the street in Kalgoorlie; in the main street. They used to go and watch him, how he used to do things. He carved all the boomerangs and you know, he was just a joy to sit and watch. And if he knew we was watching, he'd show off. He'd cock his head and smile and wink at us as if to say, 'Okay, you watch me perform here.' Oh, what a conman, we used to say. He was a smart man. Too smart. Smart talker. He'll sing out, 'Eh, you girls, come and sit with me.' Shaking hands with people. People'd chuck money in his hat. Black hat with studs in it. Twenty, ten, forty, fifty dollars. That hat was dirty because it was on the ground. So, when he get enough money, he go to that shop and buy a new black hat. He had to look nice for the tourists and when he want to go out. He used to dress up to kill. Shoes shine, the shirt and that, oh beautiful and the coat to go with it. These old Wongi fellas, they funny fellas. I had fun with them; I used to have a good laugh with them.

I don't know why everybody call him Popeye. That was just who he was. Nothing wrong with his eye; might have been, but I didn't notice. Old Popeye Johnson, I used to put his little grandchildren off to school in Kurrawang. And they all sort of grew up to know me as their big sister. I think I was lucky that way. Lot of families like that in Kal, that's why those people are really dear to my heart. They were very welcoming to a strange girl coming up from Gnowangerup and didn't know nothing, not a word of Wongi. All of these people just opened their hearts out to me. They knew I was a stranger and they thinking this one here, she's different to all the other girls. Reckon, yeah, she's from Albany, she's Noongar. 'Ah, we'll have her Wongi before long.' They done a good job, too. They knew my Dad was Wongi.

Old Popeye, he always look after us southwest girls and always make himself known to us. You'd hear him shouting coming through the gate. Sometimes you think it's a woman, but it's him, silly old man. 'Come on, darmoor no more inside,' he'd say. 'Put 'em bed out back or in front, so I watch, look after you. Tell Noongars when they come, "Nah, that's my girl, you not taking her anywhere. She's my girl, I look after her. Our family." It's marvellous now how much family I got. Hello sister.' And they cry for me. When they never seen me for long time, they sit and cry, all them Johnson girls. Only a couple left; one boy I think. Most of them all dead. And they had a big family in them days and I saw all of them grow up to be man and womans. That's something in life that I been there and done it. And the grannies, the kids now reckon, 'We know you, Mumma Loo, we know you. Helen yowa. You old boss lady.' Eldest come there with that money, put it in my hand. You not allowed to take it back, that'll break their hearts. That's the best part of being a Wongi, you can't take it back. That's yours – you keep. Most of that family taught me everything. I learnt about three languages through these old people. But even though they gone you can feel that love there in them young fellas. Wongi very gentle people. They know who you are. And I'm glad I experienced that time up there in Kal.

Old Pop Ridley, Jack Ridley, he was a loveable old man. Him and his old wife, too. She had a sweet face. He died years ago. They were at Kurrawang, outside of Kalgoorlie, about four miles. It was like my first home in the goldfields. And I enjoyed it, because it was a new experience, new place, meeting new people. And I respected them for that. My respect for them goes a long way. Two of his daughters are still going, in Kalgoorlie. I usually go and stay with them. They treat me like a big sister.

Most of the old families, most of them are all dead and gone, but I still respect their memories. The younger ones knew me and they still do. They all say, 'Auntie Helen,' or 'Didja Helen, you are one of us.' Or they sing out, 'You our Nanna.' I'll say no, I'm a Noongar. And they reckon, 'Wiyartu.' Wiyartu means, no you Wongi. I could go back now and have a good yarn with them, sit down and have a good yarn. They tell me stories about the young people, how they carry on stupid. You get a good laugh out of them. Haven't been back for about three years ago. That was for my friend's funeral. And when the family seen me there, they realise who they was talking to, the young kids say, 'Nardoo, look here. Where you come from, Auntie?' I said I come from Perth, Albany way. Your mother was my dear friend. I miss her because she was the newsreel of Kalgoorlie for Wongi people and she used to tell some funny yarns. Her name was Pearl Wells, Pearly Wells. Her old husband was a Lore man. She say, 'Ah, Helen, I know everything.'

When I went into Kalgoorlie from Kurrawang I used to work at Nindee Hostel. That's where all the kids from the outer regions, Cundeelee and Warburton,[4] all the kids come down to school. Well, I used to be there working. I used to work in the laundry then; and that was good because I enjoyed that work. This Noongar woman there. I say don't you be frightened of me. You call me Auntie. And the kids were too good. 'Auntie Helen, Auntie Helen, what we going to do?' I used to teach them life.

I drove some people home one time. We had a big station wagon. Well, it was my boyfriend's. He was a white boy. Going along, dogs and spears and boomerangs and everything you could put in it. Kids smiling at you. All you could see was their pretty smiles. Well, I enjoyed it. I took them back to Cundeelee, Laverton, Leonora. My niece Gail was up there at Cundeelee then. She was married to a Wongi boy. 'What you doing here Auntie?' she says. I said I bring all the gang back. 'What?' My sister was with me. Heather Green. And she was the best, loveliest lady, she was. Me and her were sisters. And they said come over to my house and you can rest up there. You can go early in

4 Desert settlements. Cundeelee lies 200 km east of Kalgoorlie. Warburton is 730 km from Kalgoorlie, only 230 km from the South Australian border.

the morning and you should be home by twelve. She was a very big lady, like family. And her aunties, they call me family. And that made me feel so special. I was always made welcome in Kalgoorlie. I got a name up in Kal, Laverton, Leonora.

I had a lot of them boomerangs, but I left them with my friend, and I think they've shifted now. She reckoned, 'I'll keep them for you, Auntie.' But this was the originals from old people. They used to make them and they'd sell it. Make them out of sandalwood and that's the toughest, hardest wood out. The smell of it, you can smell them anywhere in the bush.

13

Ravensthorpe Massacre

MUM'S NAME CAME from Esperance, Ravensthorpe.[5] That was terrible there, in Ravensthorpe, how they killed all our family down there, another side of the family. They never even had a chance.

The farmers around there, they didn't like Noongars. There was a lot of Dutch people, or Germans or something like that. And they used to kill all them old folk. Didn't want no blackfellas on their farms. They don't belong here. Looking at a white person, they reckon they'd have died of fright themselves. They didn't even know white people. First time they travelled through bush. That was their path. That was our down travelling way of going through from there to Albany and around the south. Poor old Noongar used to go through the bush. But white people didn't like it, blackfellas

5 https://www.noongarculture.org.au/wagyl-kaip-timeline/ See also Appendix: The Ravensthorpe Massacre

walking on their land. They were all on the sides of the hill, pointing guns; they was shooting them down like they were rabbits. Bang! Don't like you 'cause you black. Kill 'em, kill 'em, kill 'em. They nuisance! That was very sad. All they had was spears. What's a spear going to do against a shotgun? That part is still hurting. Why people do that? I don't like the colour of your skin. Kill you! Can't do anything, got to just wait for that bullet – bang! Police wasn't doing nothing about it. They was helping them, killing everybody. They hated them! Must have been frightening in them days. Look at Rottnest. I got three or four old uncles there. Grand uncles. And it hurts. That's all our family. That's what Yagan was kickin' up for. 'Why kill my family?' He was a big warrior. They never give them a chance to learn a little bit. They only know trees and nature.

Old Pop Dasborough, he was a wise old man. He used to tell me lots of yarns about the Dabs. He used to know a lot of them. They worked for him. But, I didn't know what I know now what happened on that farm. He told me everything what happened. All the massacres of my family right through the hills. All the dead Noongars there. I couldn't understand it, being a young girl. No one didn't want to take the blame for it.

Pop Dasborough was the only white man who ever done the decent thing after they shot my family. That's the hurting part. Shot my family in broad daylight, little kids and all. No one come to their aid. That was very sad. He seen the massacre that was happening down there. He used to know a lot of them, the Dabs and the Coynes, and everybody else who was with them at that time. They used to work for him till the massacre that was happening down there. He was the only bloke, him and his son, who took a shovel in the bush and buried all the family there. He picked all their bodies up, all the little children and old people and all, wipe them down, clean them all, put them in a bag and buried them properly in them graves. Buried them in open graves, covered them over, put crosses on them. He used to put rocks all over them places and all you can see now is like rocks. That's where he buried all the family, the Dabs. Well that's my mother's family. It was very cruel. If they didn't like you, you were gone. That wasn't yours to touch. You don't touch it. Our kids don't like you because you got black skin. I grew up with a lot of that. I think that's where Mum developed her fear of wadjalas. Frightened of them. Must have been terrible them days.

Later, I used to live with these old people in Albany, in West Road in Albany. Old Pop Dasborough and Mum Dasborough. Old Pop Dasborough would take me down to the farm after they finished work. 'Come on, jump in, Helen. Come to Ravensthorpe for a ride.' All them massacres of my family.

Later on in years, we went to Ravensthorpe and went to his farm in Albany, West Road. I said I'm sure I've been to this farm. And the bloke came out and introduced himself to us said he bought the farm off Mr and Mrs Dasborough. I said, 'Dasboroughs? I used to live with Dasboroughs.' I stayed with them for a while there. I was working in a shop and old people's home. I was enjoying my work that much. I had the front room. I said, 'I used to live with him and his wife. His wife was named Esther. Knew him well.' I said, 'I remember your face when you used to come for tea every now and then at Pop Dasborough's. I had the front room.' 'Oh,' he said, 'you the one used to play the piano? Helen! I remember you.' Oh, he give me a big hug and said, 'You used to like my little girl's ringlets.' I said, 'I used to comb her hair and put little bows all around it.' And she was a little doll.

Just a while ago, we went down to Ravensthorpe with Wirlomin. They got paths through the bush. Ah true, and I told them, 'No, I can't go there.' Oh, you could feel it. You could feel our family like they turning back from walking and watching you. I had that feeling that they're watching us. I said to them that I can't go there. 'You fellas can go walkabout, but I don't feel right. That's where my family was shot dead back then. That's my family's resting place.' I said to Henry, Henry Dab, my first cousin, my brother, 'You not going anywhere. Russell, you not going anywhere. That's our family. Let them rest in peace. They were running away from shotguns. Don't walk over their bodies. They're the ones that got shot. They don't need us stamping over them. You don't do that.' Well, I got this strange kind of feeling like as if they was there and I said, 'You know, I feel lifted.'

I said to all them other mob that went to the place where they was shot, 'Please don't go there, that's all my family, my mother's gang.' When they come back most of them was all very sick, weak. So, it must be something in our family's tradition. When we rest, we like to rest. And they said, 'How come you not sick?' 'It's not in me. That's my old people. I want to let them rest in peace. They don't need us around. They know we here. This is their resting ground. You don't go near them places and walk over their spirit.' That's wrong and I'm really against that. My family looking after me. I know they around. Them old people not dead; they watching you through the wind.

Now they got paths through the bush showing, hand pointing this is the way they walked. I said to my cousin, Henry Dab, look here, I don't like that. I don't feel right. It's like someone saying no, don't go there, stay here. So, I'd sit and wait for them. They had their life, what little life they had. That's their time. You can't walk over graves like that, or bones. That's wara. That's why you fellas getting sick. Can't be told. Stay away from there. That's our sleeping place. Those old people got eyes still. Their spirits will always be watching you. They know where you not supposed to go. I don't know whether I'm frightened, or else not really frightened, but that's their place, that belongs to them. Respect it. Don't walk over it, you kicking up their spirits. Wara, no good. I'm very strong against that. I got my stubbornness, but not that way.

This girl was in the bush with all the high people from up here in Perth from the government. Somewhere in that Ravensthorpe place where our people went through first, we were taught not to go there; other people can, but we can't, because that's our family there. She takes them through the Stirling Ranges. I said I hope you don't do that. Our gang strong there, very strong. Big piece of stick went right through her hip. She can't walk now. You were told not to go there. She can't hardly talk much now, it's affecting her speech. She's younger than me, my cousin. I got no time for you, girl. You been told don't go there. Our family sleep there, a resting place. They know if you a stranger. How you know, Ing? You be surprised what I know. You'll be punished one day. Her sister, big girl, she is, she looked at me, said to me: 'What you saying is true.' I said I know. I tried to tell the both of you.

14

Three wonderful fellas

THESE PEOPLE FROM Holland, Naomi and Harry Myrick, looked after Harry John when he was a baby. They were in Perth; they used to live in Riverton. They sort of looked after the little parts of his life, but I didn't know where until the Welfare people found me in Kalgoorlie. Harry Myrick died and she's over in New Zealand. She married a cattleman over there. Every now and then I see all the children. They let me know what's going on.

Then Welfare rang me. They said, 'Oh, listen, we got your son here.' He wanted to come home to me, so when Harry John was about six he came home to me in Kalgoorlie. I was still married to the Dutchman. Oh, I'm laughing, I clean forgot his name. I was able to go and pick Harry John up in Perth, where he was waiting for me. It was solid. When I looked at him, I'm thinking, ah, he's mine now. Life, that just changed like that, because I have someone myself who I can tell off, say, 'Behave yourself,' or 'Stop giggling,' if he was standing there giggling. I just loved having him home with me. This happened long before Anthony came to me. Anthony would have still been a star in heaven then, coming down, on his way down. He was a precious star up there wondering where he was going to drop next. And I must have been watching that little star, because up in Kalgoorlie you got them big stars.

Me and Harry had good times, but all of those precious little years was missing. But we got there. He learnt Noongar. I taught him. The Dutchman, my husband, he didn't accept Harry John. He had his way with him, but Harry John couldn't stand him. My husband wanted his own way, so I couldn't stay there, so we got a divorce. Quickest wedding out, four months. Four months and divorced. There was nothing there, really. I was happy for that. I'll never go through that again. And that's something I'd rather forget. But not with Harry. Harry was my boy and I wasn't going to let anyone else look after him since I got him back. If I can't do it myself, no one will. We stuck together. He knew who I was. And that's the best part, because he really come home and opened things up for me and we both really found out what mother and son was all about. We had our differences sometimes. It's natural. We got through it, worked it out. He was very strong-minded, Harry. He always come home and say, 'Sorry Mum.'

When he was thirteen, the headmaster rang me up in Boulder High School. They said, 'We got your son here, him and his brother.' I said, 'They in trouble or what?' 'I wouldn't say trouble,' he said, 'but it's a bit annoying.' He was a good old headmaster. You could talk to him like he's one of the family. And he knew Wongi kids, that's what's made him harder. And this is a little Noongar boy who would not do as he's told. Anyway, he said, 'You better come and pick Harry John up. So I had a car, drove to the school. And I went in. Well, he looked at me, put his head down, started giggling. I looked again. Steven Smith, his older brother was there! His father was a Smith. Anyway, Harry John he's making out he's looking at all the pictures around the walls. I said, 'I see the cause,' at the headmaster. 'You don't have to tell me anything. I'm taking him home and most probably brother be coming along.' Headmaster said, 'Yes, you better take them home for the day.'

Took them home. I said, 'Now, you two, you tell me what happened.' Sat them down on that chair. 'I got a wati. One old fella give me a lovely wati stick, ah, big one, too.' When anybody naughty up there they get hit. Showed me where to hit people if they giving you a hard time – shoulders, knees, ankles. That's punish stick, punishment stick. Well, I'm walking along giggling to myself. I found this wati all right. Standing at the table with this big wati in my hand. 'Now which one? Who's following who here? You kids be naughty and you getting that wati, whether you scream or not.' And that was my way of getting him straight again. I said, 'Look, I had to stand for belts and sticks and you not going to run through that door because I'm locking it.'

By then, Steven, he was shaking. Harry standing there, he was the brave one. He thought he could face me. Bang, straight across the foot, hard as I could make it. 'Would you be able to run like that? Turn the other way now, give me that other ankle.' Never cried. 'Oh,' I said, 'That not good enough, eh? Where else you want me to give it to you?' He says, 'Now Mummy, I'm sorry. Steven come to the school and picked me up and he gave me gunja.' 'Ah,' I said, 'I knew I'll get the truth out of you somehow. Steven, now where you would like it? You not my boy, but you my nephew. You don't listen to me or Auntie Maud or all those old people, you going to get the same, because I'll get Auntie Maud to do it for me. That's my big sister. And everything you boys do towards me, I'll go and tell her. I can't hit you because you with Auntie Maud all the time, but this little monkey here's not going anywhere.' He can't walk anyway. And Harry John, he limps into the bedroom. He says, 'No, I can't go nowhere because my ankle no good.' I tell him, 'I'll never hit you, but this is just a warning. Traditional punishment. Listen to me. You only got one mother. I want love coming out of you, for your teachers when you at school, or the Elders around here, because they very smart old people. That's all your darmoors and relations. You listen to them. Steven know what I'm talking about.'

And Steven, he says, 'Oh, my brother can't walk. Auntie Ing, what you done to him. He got no foot now!' I said, 'Of course he can. He got a foot stuck on his leg.' Steven, he picked him up, carried him, laid him on the bed, put his foot up, two pillows underneath. 'You right, my brother?' 'Yeah.' He's sitting there, trying to hold the tears back, that's how hard Harry was when I got him first. He was the hardest little bugger out. And I'm thinking I'll break him one day, kept telling him, 'I'm your mother. Listen to me – please. Only one mother brought you into this world and that's me.' Never said much to him for two days. He was mostly resting his feet.

Then, early next morning he come out. 'Mum, I'm sorry. I love you.' And that just lifted that burden off my chest. Well, we sat down, had a cry and hugged him. 'Now you go and have a shower, clean up, dress yourself up, go and run down and see where your stupid brother is. Don't get into trouble. I got eyes all around Kalgoorlie. They all tell me, these old Wongi. They know I'm your Mum.' He run, 'See you later, Mum.' And I felt good about that.

Only somewhere along the line, that old gunja took over and that's the downfall, I found out. He was in and out of the big house. That part was a bit hard, but he always managed to come home, ring me up, tell me he still loved me and he's coming home. Or he won't ring up for a while then he'll come home and he'll say, 'Hello Mum, I'm home,' like nothing happened. Well, we put life that way. I was pleased to see him; he was pleased to come home. We had a bit of a hard time, but we got through it – we got by. It was frightening for a while. I knew that was my big boy. I was always there for him. That's the best part of where we grew up, us two both.

Then, Harry was a street kid. He grew up to be a street kid. Even later on in his life, well and truly in his teens, he was a street kid, but he'll come home and have a weekend with me or bring his friends up, mates, and we was fine. Yeah, we had a good understanding of each other. I was a street kid with him for a while. I often go into town and stay with him. That was good fun, roughing it on the streets. This is my life. I enjoyed it. All my nieces and nephews there and, well, they loved it when I was there. I had everything. I loved every minute of it. My son was there, looking after me and why should I worry? I was divorced from the Dutchman. Isn't that lovely? I'm not ashamed of what I done. It's good. But I got sick of that life. I said, 'You're going back to your home, Fremantle, so I'm going home to Gnowangerup.' Went up and down, Gnowangerup and Albany. Travelled a bit, then come home. I got a job down there.

Harry John knew where I was. He was always coming home to me. He wanted to find out who was his family. So, I took him down. It was his Uncle's funeral. Uncle Alec Williams, my first cousin. There was people just packed in Gnowangerup. He said, 'Mum, I'm frightened.' I told him, 'Don't be frightened. You have to come and meet your father, Bill Smith,' which he did. He didn't like him from the start, took a while for him to get used to it. I said, 'He was a street kid too, like me and you.' He'd have a little laugh. He met all the gang, all the family. They said, 'Don't say that's your son!' I said, 'That's my one boy, Harry John Nellie. He's a Nellie, not a Smith.' Bill was keen to have time with him. He was pretty good, but Harry never used to stay around with him. He'd always come home to me. Later on, Bill got sick; he had pneumonia and pleurisy. He passed away a long time ago.

≈

My Anthony was born in Katanning on 29 August 1985, same day as sister Audrey's birthday. Sister Audrey is Hazel's sister. He's my grandson really. His old grandfather and his grandmother gave me him, Anthony. His old grandfather and his grandmother, they told me his mother isn't well and they can't look after him because they was getting crook themselves. He put the baby in my hands. 'I know he'd be strong with you. That's our grandson, but you're the main one for him because his mother sick.' And that's a terrible thing, but I done it.

Had his little case on the side, wasn't much, couple of rompers and nappies, that's all. Mother, she didn't buy him much. I went back to Tammin to Russell and Teresa, my brother and his wife. For a little while I stayed with them in Tammin and they give me a room for me and Tony. He was only a little fella, tired, sickly little boy he was. So, I got old Dr Gates who gave me the proper tablet, S26. 'Just a little one will do him for a while. If he got tummy ache, just give him water.' I knew that part. We learnt that in mothercraft.

So he was right, he had everything. Nappies, I didn't like them Kimby sort of things, so he had flannel nappies. That was the best. Harry was brought up on flannel nappies. And in no time he started getting bigger and bigger – never stopped growing.

Harry was locked up like a monkey in a cage in Fremantle Prison, juvenile side, when Anthony was born. We got our own flat for me and Anthony, a second-hand shop in Tammin. Well, I had the back room. At the back, there was a lovely little flat there. So, Mrs Repton, one old farmer's wife used to come in and help everybody with rations and that. She was a dear old lady. And I said, 'Have you got a room I can have here?' 'Yes, Helen, there's one in the back. It's a big room. You can put a double bed in; take it out of the second-hand shop. Cost you nothing. Mattress, big cot there on the side for Anthony.' I said, 'No, he could lie on the side of me, no worries.'

He was lying next to me and I'm in the front, aah, we lying back like king and queen. In no time, he got fat. Pretty little kid. Got all the clothes from the second-hand shop. I just used to take the clothes out if there were little clothes. She said I could have them for Anthony. Little bottles she gave me, you could boil them in a big pot, like preservatives thing. They had special stuff for my baby's bottles. That's what she was, a lovely old lady, wadjala woman, one of the farmer's wives. 'I know mothercraft,' I said. 'I used to do a lot of little kids in mothercraft, reared them up.' She reckon, 'But this little one, he's a special boy. He's going to be a charmer.' I was thinking to myself I hope you don't tell him when he grows up. We was there for nearly six months. Stayed close to Russell for a while. Go home and do all his cooking. They go to church those days. Good, solid Christian family.

Later, I went back there and saw her. She couldn't get over how handsome he was. 'Ah, this our Anthony,' she says, 'Isn't he a beauty boy?' Showed him that's where our room was in that second-hand shop. Tell him, anything you wanted from there we got. All the Noongars used to go and work for her husband, from Tammin and Quairading. And she really helped me. She was like a real old mother.

And I reared him up. All them years I missed out on Harry when he was a baby I made up with Anthony. He's my grandson really, but I'm his Mum, his Mum for life. He knows who is his mother. We've taken him down to her most of his life. As far as he's concerned, he's a Nellie. And we've been together for the last thirty years. He turned thirty the other day. We went to see him the other day, right on his birthday. My sister, that's Anthony's great grandmother, she's in a nursing home now. She's the one that gave me Anthony when he was a little baby, her and her hubby, which was my brother.

Now he's like a big giant. He didn't know any other Mum. 'That's my Mum. Mum, you my heart,' he'll say to me, even now. And he was my treasure. I grew up for another young life again. Between him and my husband's three boys, it was like growing up again, with teenagers. No, I enjoyed it.

His mother was my niece but she's good. She sort of got her life now. She's got her two girls. I got Anthony, that's the main thing. We're all happy. He's got his wife. And he'll tell everybody, 'I only got one Mum. She's the boss.' When I used to take him down to see his mother, tell him that's your Mum there, I'm your Nanna, he say, 'Mum, you Mum.'

I was on my own. I was up and down to Perth. Decided to move back to Perth and got this house in Hollybush Way, in Kelmscott and I reared my little Anthony up. Noongars was just all around, all the same southwest mob. We had good times. Started looking at boys, but didn't mess around. Anthony was a little fella, just learning to crawl. After a while I had two other boys stay with me, Darryl and Tommy. They was like two bodyguards. They were better than womans. They must have been womans before their life. That clean! Everything, spotless clean. Boys who been brought up in Gnowangerup. I seen them grow up to be men. I think jail done a lot of good for them. Anyway, they was bosses. Tommy used to cook beautiful thing and big boy, he used to make the dampers, and oh, that was just like sponge cake. So I start Anthony off on that and he started getting big himself and I'm thinking this boy getting too fat, getting heavy to carry. Tommy and Darryl, they say to me, 'We look after you, Mum.' They call me Mum, made sure the fridge was full all the time. Go down for a walk down the park, say hello to the same faces every day.

Then Harry come out of jail, together with his friend and they come around home. 'Mum, we home.' Too good. I said, 'You know who that is? This your little brother here,

Tony.' He said, 'True, Mum?' 'That's your sister's son. Auntie gave him to me to rear up. You could call him Uncle if you like.' 'Nah,' he said, 'That's my little brother.' Picked him up, carry him around, took him for rides around. He thought it was grown right up. Always had new things for him. He used to come home, when he got his pay he'd say, 'Here, Mum, a hundred dollars for Anthony. Get him some nappies and some new bottles. Don't have him drinking two or three weeks out of the same bottle. Chuck them out, get new ones, boil them up.' I said to him, 'You sound just like your father.' 'Well, he's my little brother. I got to look after him. I had training in jail.' 'But that's all mans down there,' I said. 'No,' he reckons, 'We had dolls down there. We had to wash the dolls properly.' He was a good kid. They stayed with me for a month in that crowded house and all the boys was there. Then they went their own ways. Some got married, couple I think died.

Then I met the man of my dreams, Ronald Richard Hall. I call him Orly, short for his surname, Hall. I was going through divorce. I had my divorce, but just going through rough times. Met him in Perth. We become good friends. Oh, we were friends like years ago, before any children, but that was just friends. We were star-crossed lovers. But he kept me in his head all the time. He thinking I was different to all these other girls. But I liked him. I run away from him, but he caught up with me. We got married in Quairading. So, he became my husband number two. Now I'm stuck with it. It's like a sinker that wouldn't come up and I'm trying to cut it off, but the damage is done. Ron and me have been married twenty years, thirty years now. My dearly beloved husband.

I take my life in my hands travelling with Orly. He relies on me to point him in the right direction. We drive along, me with my elbow on my hip, just pointing left, right, or straight ahead with my hand which way to go. We've ended up in some faraway places when I've waved a fly away or fanned my face with my hand. I forget I've done that and Orly keeps on following my hand. Last time we ended up in Cottesloe or Scarborough. He helps me a lot. At times I could kill him; at times he's so good. I live off his strength and he lives off mine.

Mousey, Anthony, well that's his name, Mousey, just fell in love with him. Harry give him that name, and Daniel, Ron's son. His face look like a mouse. 'Mum, you should have cut his hair,' they said, 'properly.' Little funny little face, so they called him Mousey. Ron, he sort of grew up with Noongars. Ronald's the eldest and then Darren and Daniel. Mousey's the one who brought everybody home. I always used to have kids all over the place at my house. Made sure they had something to eat, go home to their mothers and fathers. All the parents, white parents and Noongar parents knew where they was. Oh, they had their favourite auntie, Auntie Helen. Call me Auntie Helen or Mum. Now they big boys, they all married now, even the white kids all respect me as Mum. I reckon that when you achieve that, it's the best thing in life. I feel that way. I been there and done it. Yeah, all the way from that little town of Gnowangerup Mission. And that to me was one achievement. I think I'll always remember that. Yeah, but I had a good life. Good life, you know, never really got into big trouble, always there for all my boys and girls who come home, have a night and gone. Some you don't see them no more and others you grow up with them. And the kids now sort of look back on that. They reckon, 'You the best Auntie we ever had.'

I think Harry was on holidays, his first years of Fremantle Jail, when I married Ron. That big riot that time, I think him and another white boy just started that. They was only just starting to go to jail. He must have been about sixteen or seventeen. They started it. Well, all the other boys joined in; Noongars, wadjalas and Wongis. Next minute they's all on top of the roof. Old Freo burning. Yeah, he was a rough cowboy, Harry. He pulled through that. I said, 'Don't ever do that again little boy.' 'No, Mum, but it was good fun. Before, it was like everybody was walking around half dead.' He told me after, 'This wadjala boy, my friend, we talked for weeks. He said to me no, he don't want to do it. I said to him don't worry brother, I'll be with you.' Harry was in there long enough he learnt the trade. But he was honest about it. He said, 'Mum, I done it. I done my time. Don't judge me.' But I always loved him when he come home. He's a part of my blood, the main part. He's boss. My one and only son.

Anthony, he's thirty now. We had fun over the years. Anthony comes to see me when he can. 'I had to come and see you, old Mum.' He's got his mother. but she had that much strokes, her voice just completely went on her. She's younger than me. She'd be about the same age as my baby sister.

Now, we go and see him at the big house. He's on holiday for four years – tried to be a big shot. Last time I put him in there. Maybe he'll learn somewhere along life's highway. He'll be well and truly 34 when he gets out. He's in Wooroloo now. He can come home for a day and then go back to the prison, play football, cricket, that's the best part of it, we can see him more often. I even say to Anthony now those words that Miss Hipwell said to me: 'Always remember, be sure your sins will find you out.' 'Mum, why you talking to me like that for?' I tell him, 'You know why, because I love you. Sometimes it helps to talk to Him up there, say sorry.' 'I sure do love you, Mum.' I miss him.

Orly, he hates beer. He don't like it because he used to be the worstest drunk out. Used to be a bikie. Oh, big head there. He drifted on his own before I met him. Must have been a terrible life. Fast – too fast. He never talks about it. He had a terrible accident, motorbike accident. Nearly killed him. Legs, back. He was in hospital for a long time. But, he survived. He lost a lot of memory of that, anyway. I don't think he wants to bring that back. I didn't know him then. I'm glad I never went through that with him.

Took him years to get him to wash his hands. Put a little bit of soap on his hands and wash it. Too much effort to get a towel. That's why I had to teach him like he was a little kid. So, it's hard. And he wasn't a bloke to be taught. Oh, he'd take me flying out the door, me and all the kids till I had enough of it. I told him, 'Straighten your ideas up or else I go. I'll grab Anthony and we'll go.' But the boys was crying – his sons. 'No Auntie, you can't leave us. You better than Mum. Mum don't know how to look after us. We're too much of a burden to Mum. You, we can stand and argue with you.' 'Yeah,' I say, 'You might try, but you don't stand over me. You can go just so far enough, but then you stop.' 'And that's why we like you.' But Darren he always says, 'I love you, Mum.' My Elvis Hall. I call him Elvis Hall. He working on the mines up north now. I hope he's still got the job because they're sacking the lot of them, eh?

It's sad, very sad, but they didn't see their own Mum when they was little kids. I think she was frighten to raise kids, because she always say to me, 'They your boys. You mother. You give them your love.' But these boys, Daniel and Anthony, they're like brothers. They stand like two big elephants. Bony M is Darren. Ronald, well I call him Hopalong Cassidy. They all got their names. They look at me like I'm a second mother. Even Noongars come and tell me, 'Have you seen your son?' I go, 'Which one?' 'Oh, Daniel or Darren.' Darren, I couldn't hide from Darren. He know every little place I go. But Anthony, he the boss – and they all know that.

They look back in their lives, now, the boys, all his sons. They'll say, 'You our Mum. You seen us grow up. We got our Mum in Lockridge.' We had fun. And Orly never used to like it because every time he argued with me, the boys will start on him. 'Come on Dad, slow down. That's Mum.' Yeah, even now. That was good. Anthony was always my baby. He had his silly ways, but I didn't care. Harry was the same, 'You boss old woman, you.' Noongar way of talking. 'My motherrrr,' Harry used to say. And he used to stand there with no shirt on, arms out wide, 'I got the best motherrr.' And everybody used to see him and that used to give me a boost, hear your kid saying things like that.

But life became a bit too tough for Harry. Years later when we was living in Swan View, I told him, 'You go to the doctor, because I got a feeling you got something wrong with your legs.' No, he wouldn't go to this silly doctor. Wouldn't show me. He lying with his shorts on one day. I just picked the rug up and looked. All down his legs, sugar. Sugar sores! He wouldn't tell anyone and I could see how he walked. He wouldn't get tablets for it. And I think life was getting a bit tough for him. That's my eldest son, Harry.

Losing my only son, that's another heartache. I'm still living with it. He come in one day. 'Mum, wash my clothes out.' So I washed his clothes out, hang them all up. I knew he was on the hard stuff because this business down there on his legs was making it hard for him. Anyway, he went to Albany, come back, had time with all the family, his cousins and that.

Then he said, 'I'm going to Fremantle, Mum.' Asked him, 'When you coming home?' 'Ah, Mum, I'm right, I own the streets. I'm a street kid now.' So I knew where he was. Could always go see where he was. But that was the last time I saw him. Died from an ice overdose two o'clock in the morning.

Up in Swan View, I said to my husband, 'Ron, let's go. Let's go to Fremantle and get a burger.' Now I look back it must have been the same time as he died. Beautiful burger, and I ate all mine. Usually I leave half, put it away and eat it later. This time I ate it. Never even known about it. 'That's funny, I ate all that burger there.' Ron said, 'How you feel? You feel all right?' I said, 'Yeah, I feel great.'

Next day the police came, told Daniel, that's Orly's son that I reared up, to get a chair, put me on that chair, sit down in the armchair. Orly's other son, Ronald, he was there. And we yarning like nothing happened and he said, 'How are you, Mrs Hall?' I said, 'Pretty good. I been there and done it, whatever you want to ask me.' It was a beautiful day, just like this one. He didn't know how to come out with it at first. 'Is Harry your son?' I said, 'Yes, I known Harry all his life because he's my son.' He said, 'You know, Mrs Hall,' – he sat right in front of me, held my hand. I think, this is strange. I said, 'Tell me straight out. I know something's wrong.' He said, 'We found Harry this morning, at two o'clock in the morning in Stuart Street in Fremantle. We found him dead at two o'clock this morning.' I said, 'It couldn't be two o'clock,' I said, 'I was in Fremantle at two o'clock. Me and my husband went from here to Fremantle and I ate a full burger by myself.' Well, everybody just looked. It never hit me at first. I never realised what's happening. All of a sudden, life, and everything within it, cut off. Click. My ears just shut off. All my whole body just clicked off. I just sat there. I'm looking at your face but I couldn't remember your name. They talking, I could see them moving their mouth. Clicked off. I just cut myself off from the world.

Oh true, I'd never want to go through that sort of thing again, because after Mum and Dad, that was hard. He was my only son. He was the eldest. He was older than Orly's boys. And they all were tongue-tied themselves, they couldn't even talk to me, because I was listening to nothing. I automatically clicked off. I think it was the shock of him going. Shock can do that to anyone. That was hard. If anything can give me toughness in life, that was it. I just lost everything.

Families come from everywhere, southwest, nor' west, goldfields, say sorry, because everybody knew him. People come and talk to me, all the family. Never heard it. Sat and looked. Ron, he used to say to them, 'Don't stay too long with her.' But I come good. Wise – and real independent.

Harry, he was one of the kindest boys in Perth, he always looking after his old mates, saying, 'Don't worry, I'll bring a bottle of wine back for you.' And even now the old men tell me in Perth when I go to town just to visit places that used to be close to him, 'We lost our best mate; your son.' That was Harry. I was lucky to have him for 22 years. Same age as Toono when he died. My son died when he was 22, nearly twenty years ago. That's why I hate ice [crystal methamphetamine]. I know he's still beside me.

When I lost my son, I didn't care. Even now, I get that strange feeling. Even if you try, you can't stop longing to hold him. Always keep him in my memory. We buried him home in Gnowangerup with Mum and Dad. So, he's right. We go down every so often, clean his grave. We went down a couple of weeks ago. Lovely trip. I thought he was going to run off the road a couple of times, poor old Orly. Some of the things we get up to, that's why I love travelling with him, just for a laugh sometimes. That's why I love my little brother. It would have been too much money for me and Orly to pay for his funeral in Gnowangerup. I wanted him to be buried in Kojonup, next to his own father. But my brother done everything for me, said, 'Put him home with Mum and Dad.' And I never had no say to that. He paid for everything. It was hard – and sad. That's all my memories and dreams, they all just flopped. I lost my best little mate, my fighting mate, my arguing mate. Trying to stand over me, I took him flying with a mop. And that's the second time I really hurt. Mum and Dad come back into view. They were there with me.

Yeah, that's the sort of life I had. He was my treasure. Precious, precious treasure. And nothing will ever bring him back. The pain will always be there. Same sort of pain I had when I lost Mum and Dad. But I was that frightened to talk. I just kept it all in my heart. Over the years I felt like I'm stuck here and I want to get it out but I can't. Don't know how to. Shy, like Mum. But now, I taught myself to move on. If you feel a tear in your eye, let it go. You don't need it. The sunshine is warmer than a tear. There, my big boy, just rest easy. I will always love you, Harry – forever.

I miss Anthony. I'll be glad when he can come home. Since I lost my son, I need someone like him around. We both miss Harry. He always looked up to his big brother. He was really his Uncle, but he used to call him his big brother. He really miss his big brother. That's the way I've taught him to respect, especially your big brother, I used to tell him. We got on well, us three.

Yeah, Anthony, he looks at them other boys, 'You don't know my mother. My mother is boss.' Yeah, I know it. Ah, that was good. It's lovely to have that sort of gift. I got little ways I know things. And I love that. That's my Uncle give me that. I don't give nothing to no one. Only for myself and my family. My boy used to say to me, 'Mum, what you do? How you know this is going to happen?' And he used to listen to me. I tell him, 'You'll know. Anything happen to me, you'll know it.' Before I used to get worried. He used to ring me up from jail. 'Mum, now don't you get upset. I heard all about it.' I can hear him saying, 'That old woman, silly old woman, how come she knows?'

My little grandson now, Anthony, little Anthony, he's in Albany. He'll tell his mother, walk in the kitchen if she's cooking: 'My Nan coming down today.' Couple of days before I get there he knows. She'll be sitting there just smiling at me. I say, 'What happened?' 'I knew yesterday you'd be down.' You see I give him that all by myself. 'He knows, he knows when you coming down.' I know when Russell's around. It's like a cyclone. We have a good laugh at each other.

Even Anthony has a visit in jail. He tells me, 'Mum, when I wake up I feel there's someone sitting on the end of my bed.' I say to him, 'That's your brother, Harry John, and don't be frightened of that. He's always with me and you.'

15

Family

I LOOK BACK over the years and that slowly came to me how much they put me through, Native Welfare and old missionaries. Being taken from my Mum and Dad and put into the Mission, that will never leave me. I've got it set in my heart. It's like a tattoo that can never be washed away. That's the part of my life that I'm trying to grab and put it back. But you can't. It's like the wind, go right through you. That, I'm hurt about. Still hurts. I never, ever want to go through that again, but it's a memory that will stick in my mind for the rest of my life. I was afraid of them. They took me in the Mission. You have to do what they tell you. That's their rules. We had to listen to everything. 'You want to be a Noongar or wadjala, white person?' That's what I hated. 'Stop those other Noongar ways and learn discipline. You not on no reserve now. Forget about your language.' And that was hard. All the years it stuck in my mind and I hated that. But for them I might have still have had a Mum and Dad.

Where our Mission was, they had a big old board that said: United Aborigines Mission Gnowangerup. That's my home. I thought it was going to be my home forever. It wasn't really a dull Mission. At the time, we thought it was because we were still learning facts of life. I'm glad I had that. I hated it at the time, but I'm glad I been there; and I look back on the years now and I look up to the Lord and I'll say thank you for them wonderful people who taught us. Thank you for bringing us through. And it gives me a beautiful joy. Just get up and walk around smiling. And it was good. I never thought so at the time, but it's a blessing.[6]

In a way, I'm happy I had that life in the Mission. I was sort of like a black-skinned woman living in a white way. I made a lot of wonderful mates and friends, family. We still together, Mission kids, doesn't matter how old we are, how far we come in life. Knowing who we are and knowing where we come from; that little Mission in Gnowangerup. And I think that was the best part. It made me who I am. Ing Nellie, daughter of George Nellie and Tilda Nellie.

Now, we're grandparents ourselves. We all have time together, you know, kids who've been through the Mission and we knew what we all went through. Always knowing you my sister, we been brought up together. That's a bond it'll never go away, I think. That's the best part of it. We had

---

6 Blessing has a different meaning in Aboriginal English. In the context of this sentence, it could mean 'something that was'.

someone to talk to, someone to laugh and fight with. And you don't forget it. I look back now and think that might have built my confidence up. We all knew each other. Years later we all used to get together, have a good drink-up party, tell our kids, 'Ah, this is my sister. Grew up in the Mission together.' When us Mission mob together little grannies say, 'That's my nan, that's my nan'. 'Yes, we all your nans. We Mission mob.' 'See, I told you that's where my nan comes from,' proud that her nanny a Mission girl. I look back on them precious years; I tell the girls, look, if you went through what I went through you must have something special in your heart. I know I got my Mum's heart and I'm keeping it, through my Uncle Malcolm. My little granddaughter, she's a little show-off when she's around me. Her mother and her own grandmother will say, 'Crystal, Nanna don't want to hear that.' She thinks it's the best thing in her life. 'I got the best Nanny in Albany.' And the other kids all look at her and go, 'No, she our Nanna, too.' And that's a little part of happiness that comes my way.

Lot of little grannies come around, pull me on the dress. I pick them up and cuddle them. Little Anthony will stand there, say, 'That's *my* Nan.' 'You got to share her with us, that's our Nanna, too,' they'll say. Little kids, I have a good yarn with them, listen to them what they talk about. 'Ah, come on,' I'll say to them. 'Run! – First one on my lap.' We have good fun. When I want to sneak him off from school, I just show my face in Albany. When he know I'm there, well he'll meet me at the bus stop. He's supposed to go to school. We go down to Albany town and have our McDonald's Big Mac, ice cream and all, we have a good feed. Then I tell him come on now, Nanna will catch a bus home so you can go to school. I give him his twenty dollars. I gave all the other kids ten dollars each. The kids know. They say, 'Nanna, how much you gave Tony?' 'Ten dollars.' 'No you never. We know.' And I thinking be sure your sins will find you out. And that stuck with me over the years and I love that. Thank you Miss Hipwell, wherever you are. I know she's in heaven.

And I'm looking at little nieces and nephews running around, following me everywhere, like an old mother hen. Mother Goose. That's how I felt. I tell those little kids, 'I'm going to go away from here as far away as I can.' 'Why, Auntie?' 'Away from you little treasures. Auntie Ing going to run away from you.' They run and tell their mother, 'Auntie Ing going to leave us.' Their mother say, 'She not going anywhere. Staying right with you. Don't listen to her – only wishing.'

When I was in the Mission I found out Mum and Dad, they had fifteen other children before us, all buried somewhere in Gnowangerup. If only a few of them would have lived it wouldn't have been so hard, but that's something I learnt to live with, got on with it. But it's still there. No one can never take that away from me. Lots of other kids, their father and mother, half of them had all finished up. And that's what I couldn't understand, too. How come they split up? They were so happy. How come Mum and Dad stuck together? They died together, left us with the name of Nellie. And that's a strong hold on me and I'm keeping that forever.

At the moment, I wouldn't want to be anywhere else. I been there and I done the worst part of my life, all the ups and downs I had. Now, life has been good to me. I'm just thankful to be here. I look back and I'll say, 'Well thank you, Lord, thank you my old people.' I can feel them standing beside me, pushing me on. There's someone there pushing me on. I'll find it. I know who it is. I got my Auntie's name, Ellie Nellie, who delivered me. That's who and what I stand for. Myself. No one going to change that.

I had good times and I remember when I was a little girl on the Borden reserve – that's a cherished time. But, the good times never lasted long. You're happy and you enjoying life and some tragedy will come up. I was cut down. The worst time was when I lost Mum and Dad. Found out they won't be coming back any more. Died on the road six miles out of Narrogin. I really and truly felt on my own. I had this little boy and a baby girl, so I had to be there for them, my baby sister and little brother. So, I thinking if Mum and Dad not here, I got them. We Nellies. Try and tell them who they are. I think, why this happen to me? Doesn't anyone like us?

I look at my photo and I think, well Mum must have looked something like that. I think I'll get dressed up in an old-time dress or something and get a portrait done of myself and then get dressed again and get it into nowadays. And there, you got me and Mum, because she must have looked something like me. No one wouldn't know, only us two. Ah dear. Old aunties used to say, 'You the spitting image of your Mum.' She must have been a good-looking lady, eh?

I never saw a photo of my little sister, Hilary. But just a little while ago me and my friend went to the library in Perth. We was looking at photos of the old Gnowangerup Mission and they got a photo of my little baby sister, Hilary. That was sad. It catch my heart. I felt awful – of what happened them days. Just cried my heart out when I saw her. It was worthwhile going through; I just felt like having tears right there. I never seen a picture of her before. So precious. Most of them kids in that picture there is gone, dead, but there's a few of them around and they got their own lives, and some of them are good, some of them are no-hopers. But you get them in all sides of races, ana? No I just felt down in the dumps. Thinking back, my memory went right back to that time when they took that photo, 'cause we was standing way over, watching them, otherwise they would be running out to us. They weren't allow to come out of that yard. They were like little lost sheep. When they finally did, they run to me. All my life I had something to do with children. I love that. When I saw that photo, ah, I cried. My little sister, little one I used to carry around. And I was left with two of them, Russell and Hilary. For years I used to say, 'Why me, Mum?' Couldn't understand. It's still a heartache now.

I love painting. I'll think of a thing and I'll draw it straight out. I can stand and look at the scenery and just draw it. Not think of it until I put the colours in. That's a gift – I've always had that. I use oil paints and a wash one. Watercolours. But I like oil ones. You can mix them in together, all them beautiful colours. And I draw Gnowangerup Mission from the memories I got of that Mission. But I'd like to get canvas and do them properly with my little memories before my memories go on me. All of the old buildings have gone, only one old place down in the bottom. I think that's still there. The rest of it's all gone. Gnowangerup will always be a special part of my life – the Gnowangerup Mission. I'd love to get it back, but I can't. I drawed some pictures; it was like everything was there, all just coming to my pencil and I just drawed it. That old Mission life. Yeah. But even now when I go back to where Gnowangerup Mission was I could almost feel the kids there, you know, feel faces looking at me, shadows. You can hear things. I think maybe now I'm getting older it's all starting to affect me and that's a sad time. I get away, have my little tears and that, sit on my own for a while, feel better. You can almost see the shadows of the kids running around. It's so real. That's my memories.

When the Mission closed and I went onto the Gnowangerup reserve, if I didn't want to do anything, oh, I'd be stubborn. But old people knew what I needed. I'm very thankful that I was able to listen to them before they went and left me. What them old people done for me back in them days – powerful, very powerful. I think I was blessed that way. And I can still hear Uncle Malcolm saying it.

'Hey, little girl, you not old enough yet. You listen.' He was a strong influence in my life after I lost Mum and Dad. He could see things that I can't. He was my treasure, he was like a Dad to me and I'll always have him, doesn't matter what I do and where I go. I think Dad knows that, too.

I sit back and think now that Uncle Malcolm he was preparing me, because he knew what was going to happen to me in years ahead and he didn't have much time to live, so it was his place to tell me things. Auntie Ellie was the same. But Uncle Malcolm, I knew him and he knew who I was and that's the best part of where I am today. I'm at a place where I can sometimes forget the past, but my memory always gets me upset, a little memory of anything that anyone done wrong to me, I'm finding that out very hard sometimes. But I can get by. I got this far and I'm not giving up. He was a special old man. I used to call him Dad, and he taught me things that well, I look back now from the time I went back to the reserve. I didn't know how to live on the reserve. He used to tell me in a little gentle voice, 'Hey, I'm your Uncle. You want to find out things, you come to me.' And that to me is the greatest love any Uncle can give his daughter. And he did, and I knew then I was special to him.

16

Black and white

I BEEN BLESSED[7] with other way of living, wadjala way. And that's a sad part of my life. You know for years I had that hate. Hate there, in my heart. Really hurting hate. I couldn't seem to get rid of it. I had a strange feeling that I'm a Noongar – but I got a wadjala mind. I got to get rid of that. That's not for me – I'm a Noongar. People used to say things. I know what they meant. They were lucky they didn't get a fight. But I learnt to stop that. Even amongst my own gang, telling me how to live. I had enough of that in the Mission. My family used to say to me, 'You not a wadjala, nah, you Noongar, yeah. But stop being a flash Noongar.'

7 Blessed has a different meaning in Aboriginal English. In the context of this sentence, blessed is more one of acceptance of something that has happened, with more of a negative connotation than the literal meaning. Raised in a Christian mission, Ing would have learned the literal meaning early in life in addition to that spoken in Aboriginal English.

A few times in shops it was really embarrassing. Albany, in Katanning, anywhere, we had to wait while white people was served first, even if we was there before them. What we got to wait for them? They told us white people got to go first. And I never felt so shamed in my life. That was a disgusting, horrible time in our life. 'Wait until the white people go first.' But we were privileged; we were allowed to go in after them. I didn't understand that because half of them little kids that was served before me was my friends at school. And you have a little kid come up and say, 'You not allowed to take that.' We were looking at it! This was one time in Gnowangerup. I said, 'Why I not allowed to touch it? I'm not stealing it. I got my own money.' 'Because you black.' That little girl got a hiding – hiding of the day. I punch her up and down. 'Don't you dare say that to me! I'm from the Mission. I'm proud of who I am.' We became good mates over the years. She come and told me, explained it to me, 'My mother doesn't like blacks.' And I said to her, 'But that's not you. Your mother's not you. You got to be yourself. We got a place here.' And she said, 'Yeah, I know.' Father was good. He used to make sure we all play happy. It's just the mother – and the grandmother. She's a very hard old woman.

Gnowangerup, sometimes they'd just serve us to get rid of us. Other shops wouldn't even serve us at all. Tell us to go away because we black. 'Don't worry about it. You always got a window,' we used to say. That's how cheeky I was, me and my little niece, Melva, Anthony's grandmother. And we run away laughing, 'You always got a windowwww.' I'd say to Melva, 'Don't stay here. These white people all painted with the same brush, same colour – white.

They were good days of learning in the sixties. There was a lot of hatred towards us, especially kids that weren't from the Mission. 'I wouldn't be able to serve you because you not from the mission.' 'Can't swim in the swimming pool, only the Mission children.' So, we was privileged that way. Other kids had to swim in a dam. Don't know why they wasn't allowed in the swimming pool. Hot day and those reserve kids told, 'You got to be from the Mission to swim in the swimming pool.' Mission kids got treated like half wadjala.

Nowadays, not so much of that sort of thing. I know I can get what I want without explaining myself. But sometimes I explain to the lady if they serving the white people first, because there's always someone who run in and buy something and go. I'll say, 'Excuse me, I was here first.' Get it over and done with. That's what I say to them. But now, it's more equal. Even the kids, wadjala kids are always with the Noongar kids. We never had that in the sixties. Weren't allowed to.

All my life I been at this place where there's always someone taking things off me and I can't seem to get my hands on what's mine. Who am I? They took all my IDs off me, everything I ever owned, which was not much. Well, I had two ways, whether to go wadjala way or Noongar way, so I kept with the wadjala way. I reckon I sickened all them people. Everything I see what they eat and I go, 'Eww, yuck, I don't eat that!' You know, little things like that. And they used to be like throwing flour on me or some meat or something. 'You come down to our limits.' And I found out who was my cousins and who weren't. 'You don't have to be like that. You not a wadjala. Come down to our standard.' I said, 'I don't like it.' I thought to myself, I'm not staying around here, there's too much prejudice in my own family. I can't live with that, so I got out, travelled a little bit. But now I'm glad I had that life on the reserve because I know a lot now, little things in life, just being myself. I feel within myself completely comfortable. I had wonderful guardian angels. My love will always be there for my elderly Noongar family because they taught me how to be myself. And it's a great feeling.

Later I used to hate white people come up to me and say, 'You should be doing it this way.' I think, hey, I had that in the Mission. I don't have to live with it. I'm Ing Nellie. Stop it! That's when I get wild and I tell them what I think of them and walk off. It took years to get over that. I had to do something. They was taking control over who we are. I'm Noongar and a proud Noongar at that. But now they telling me how to live my life: different friends, teachers, all wadjalas. No way. I had enough of that in the Mission; just walk off. And that was hard for years after. That's a part there I'm sad about, yeah. At that time of my life there was things going on in Gnowangerup that I wasn't aware of, people's deaths and things. Everything in my life was missing; always used to throw that at me. 'Ah, you don't know nothing.' But the oldies made it up to me and that's why I feel so strong now. It was a bit of a jigsaw puzzle sometimes. You don't know whether you're coming or going half the time, but in my own mind, I knew where I was going. Hey slow down, this is Ing.

17

Old friends

I HAD A lot of special people in my life, people who helped me through difficult times, helped me find out who I was. One of the best was my nephew, Ronnie Williams.[8] His mother's my first cousin.

Ronnie, he was with Dad when he died. Then he went travelling. Leave all his family in Kalgoorlie. He fell in love with a girl in New York City. He met her through a friend in Kalgoorlie, two old people, Mr and Mrs Douglas, and they used to look after us too at the Mission. They were absolutely beautiful. Little short people. He was in Gnowangerup for a while. He used to give us lollies every time he come down to the Mission. Ronnie became a preacher. They told him about this girl having problems way over there in New York.

8 http://www.smh.com.au/articles/2003/11/23/1069522469366.html?from=storyrhs
http://www.focalpoint.org.au/archive-ai&a-articles-ronwilliams.php

All that street, that big city, skyscrapers. The first time he been there. He just stand singing, 'Hello brother,' that's how he talk, singing talk. 'My name Ronnie Williams, I'm from Australia.' Ah, he was a doer. Get a good laugh out of him.

They went back to the goldfields, married the girl from over in New York City, Diane. She said everybody knew him by the time he left New York. I think she was a big lady that gets all heaps of money. Business lady. Yeah, one of those people. Yeah, she told me, 'I had everything – gold if I wanted to, diamonds. I was a top lady in New York City,' she said. 'I had everything. This one bloke from the desert jumps out of the blue like a blown-away leaf off a tree, playing his gospel music. Little man from Kalgoorlie, Western Australia goldfields.' She said, 'I couldn't seem to get him off my mind. Everybody loved him. And I left the beautiful part of New York to come here to live in a cave. Didn't know what kangaroo meat was until I ate it. Didn't know what damper was. I had luxury things.' People gave him things.

Ronnie, he'd ask the Lord if he can have some things. Even the Flying Doctor, they wanted to give him money, but he said, 'No, I live off the land. Marloo, big red kangaroo, emu.' These kangaroo fight. Big boomers they very protective, they kill womens and men. Never even been on the dole. He reckon, 'That's the work of the devil.' He stood on his own foot, praying to the Lord Jesus. He lived off the land, goanna, kangaroo, emu, now and then bush turkey. Never starve. And he look so solid with it.

They got married in a cave on the other side of Leonora. He was a clown in a way. They went about ten miles down the road to where this cave was and that was their little honeymoon spot. In the morning it was beautiful, in the evening was beautiful. 'We had mattresses,' she said to me. 'That was nice enough. Lie back and watch all the beauty, the sun coming up and after when the sun going down.' Two dogs they had, so they wasn't on their own.

And from New York City to Kalgoorlie, to the goldfields. When she came over she said she didn't know what a kangaroo look like, only through pictures. He come home one day and just plonked a kangaroo down in front of her. From white to the desert. But from New York to there, she didn't know what she was in for. Look back now, you can sit back and have a laugh. But it was a whole new experience for her. When I seen her she was lovely and white, come back like a blackfella, her skin. And she turned around to her sister-in-law and she said, 'What am I in for? He's a bushman.' By the time he married Diane, she was telling me, 'Auntie Helen, I didn't even know a thing about the bush till I met your nephew. I don't know if he wanted to teach me Wongi, Noongar or what. By the time six month went by I knew every little branch on the tree; I know where to pick that fruit off.'

Then Ronnie, he went to heaven. And he was never a skinny bloke, he was always a big bloke until he got sick. He was sick for a long time. Too much travelling and I think age was catching up with him. He would have been in his early 60s. He was a mighty man, my nephew.

I was in Perth or Albany. They said you got to go to Kalgoorlie. I got to find somehow to get up there. But my nephew give me the price to get the bus and then the train up. And I went into the church and, ah, you could feel the presence there, something, the Lord, heavenly host was there. See all these big men standing in their costume from where they come from. Big notice of where they from and who they are. Stood very strong for their country. And they had the flags from their country. Our little kids had the Australian flag, Union Jack.

They came from four corners of the earth. And inside the church was all yellow rags, but tied up to seats because he was a God-sent person, you know like a prophet. But he was a simple bloke. They had for every seat a bottle of water on it. And in the front we had yellow and red, that's his family only in the front. Diane, she was on her own, her and her little girl, Lydia. Well, when Lydia seen me she come and grabbed me, 'Nanna, come and sit in the front with Mum.' Diane, she said, 'I've been blessed. I've had enough tears. Everyone from all over the world here.'

And people did come from all round the world for his funeral. It's marvellous, people's love for Ronald. They held up all the truck roads, the police force, all for Ronnie. And all our family was behind him and I looked back and you couldn't even see the end of the road, the traffic. Had to go very slow right through to the cemetery. All of Kalgoorlie was there, those people from north, south, east and west, from every corner of the world. He was a gentle, humble man. He wanted the people to know he loved the Lord.

I told her, 'Diane, you a strong woman. I love you forever. You my niece-in-law. I won't give you up.' And everybody in that hall, two days his coffin was there, everybody could see. You walk in the door and there was big tables there full of fruit and bread, fresh bread, for people who were travelling long way. Bag of food there, take it. If you're hungry, it's yours. And water. He was a powerful man. They buried Ronnie Williams in Kalgoorlie.

But I couldn't get over that big African man. Negro blokes who got gold on their hands, gold chains. Oh brother, he had this big row of rings. They was packed. He said, 'This is nothing. I just wear this because I miss the other rings.' One big bloke told me, 'You know what, sister? I was top pin. Everybody give me money otherwise they get the bullet. I'm a hit man.' He was one of those. 'Yes, you don't do what I tell you, you'll die.'

Anyway, he said, 'I had the world at my feet I thought, until I met Ronnie Williams. He's my brother. He made me stop, turn around and look at myself in the mirror. All I could see was a man's shell. Inside was eating me. I didn't know how to get rid of this hatred until I met Ronnie. I took that little blackfella's hand,' he said. 'It was that tiny in mine, for a man. And he showed me the way.' He said, 'I just gave everything away – to my family, around the street, to people I hated after I gave my life to the Lord Jesus. I don't know if they lived in luxury or not, my cars, give them away to come to Australia. The money, I was earning thousands. This little old Aboriginal bloke was singing on the street in New York City. And people just come there and talking to him, giving him coffee, giving him tea. And I come from New York City right to Kalgoorlie cemetery.' And three or four blokes from America, India, North America Indians, all dressed in their costumes and England. Iceland people! They was there dressed in their costumes.

Ronnie and Diane stayed married until he died. Diane's in Canberra now. She's my niece-in-law. One daughter they had, Lydia and she's beautiful. She's in all them big sporting things around the world. Diane never did go back to New York. She made her home in Canberra. Lost contact with Diane. Don't know how to get in touch with her. I'd love to talk to her again.

I still laugh my head off when I think about Ronnie preaching. Ah no, we all used to go to funeral. That was the worst time in Gnowangerup. Hot day. Poor old fellas. And Ronnie preaching to everybody that life is this, life is that, if you go the right way God will be there. Talking for hours. And talk, all the old people whispering, 'Tell him, c'mon, hurry up, hurry up.' Nah, that was Ronnie. Then one would keel over. We was stupid. Stand back, have a good giggle. Then another poor old Noongar would keel over, head on chest. Ended up there was all these old Noongars, pfthhh, flaked out all around. He didn't care, he didn't care, so long as he could preach about the Lord. One of the boys used to get up, 'Excuse me Uncle Ronnie, everybody all fainting here, the sun is too hot for their heads.' And Ronnie say, 'I'm sorry, I'm sorry, I just got a little bit more to say.' Noongars used to turn around and walk off. No, I never was so embarrassed. 'Brother Ronnie, can you hurry up, please? Too hot. We need a drink of water.' Ah, true. 'Yes, I'll be over in a minute,' he sing. Another hour we was still standing there half asleep. We had funny times.

Another time, my old Uncle and Auntie going through the bush. Uncle Otchie and Auntie Dorothy. Horace, his name was, but we called him Daddy Otch and we called Auntie Dorothy Auntie Dolly. Well, they killed two karrda, bungarra, big goanna. That's a beautiful big fella, killed him, two of them for dinner. His wife was way out here and he was here. Little skinny man wearing bell-bottom trousers. He was going along and we was behind him coming. Kids all with us. Anyway, we was halfway home, past Tambellup and coming back to Gnowangerup. And he said, 'Dolly'. 'What?' 'You killed that karrda?' 'Of course I did!' she said. 'He's dead now. He's not showing his eyes.' She'd knocked him in the head, thundered him. 'Dolly, you sure you did?' 'Yeah, I killed him.' 'Are you sure? What's this pinching my leg here?' He had legs like bone! Boniest little legs. 'Dolly, I think he got my bone.' Well, there was no meat there so that karrda had to hold onto something with those big claws, poor fella. She said, 'No, I killed him. You seen me kill him!' 'No, you never, Doll, he's sittin' here. Can you feel it?' That karrda, he was stuck to this poor old fellas leg. Well, he must have come to, this karrda, this goanna, come to life again and wonder what's wrong with him, what's happening. He must have crawled up inside the trousers, get warm most probably, poor thing. He was stuck to this old man's leg and he wouldn't let go for nobody.

Ah, poor old fella. Well, Auntie Dolly, she starts hitting that karrda inside Uncle Otchie's trousers. She must have hit him that much times, I'm sure she nearly broke the poor fella's leg. Ah, true. That karrda must have been bruised, but he still hung on, clung to that poor old man's leg, never had any meat on it, it was just bones on his leg. And she's hitting away at this poor karrda and he could feel this thing coming up and up, don't know how she was missing it, but all she was doing was bashing his leg. 'Ah Dolly, Dolly, help! Don't go any higher. I don't know if I got legs, or what.' Well, this karrda he was sticking all right. Must have had his kneecap. That didn't worry the old girl. She kept giving it to him with the stick. He kicked and got one side of his trousers off, but the karrda sort of stuck on the trousers with his claws still dug into his kneecap. When she realised what was going on, she said, 'You got no pants on! Get them shorts! Wadjalas coming along.' I don't know if they was taking photos or what. Funny old lady; she was big old fat lady. Dolly Yorkshire.

Old Dolly. Dolly that was in that photo from the Mission, that's her Auntie. Well, talk about laugh! And the poor old fella, he never walked for a full week after. Should have rubbed that karrda down with goanna oil or something. He'd automatically fall off. But nup, she done a good job.

Sister Audrey, Hazel's sister, she was another old angel. This old girl getting down and down and her grandchildren was giving her problems. I really felt for her. She was battling to survive. She didn't know how to tell them kids to slow down. I was there for her. She'd have her little tears and go back to brother Lomas. I look up to Lomas like a big brother, first cousin. Audrey's brother. Anyway, she was up here in Perth and I said to brother Lomas, 'Where my chook?' 'Oh, you never heard?' he said. 'She's in Sir Charles Gairdner.' 'What for?' 'That flu she had, that wasn't flu, that was cancer. We didn't even know. She's close to me, too. Never even told us.' Well, it's like everything just shoved all at me at once. Didn't know what to do.

So, we got a late night call from Albany Regional Hospital to get down there. She sent for us, me and my brother. She was saying where Ing and Russell? Audrey was lying in Albany Regional Hospital. We went to see her before she died. She had cancer. That utterly shocked me. You know, over the years she was my big sister. She not going to leave me. She never told me she had cancer.

Russell came around here to pick me up. 'Come on,' he said. 'I'm taking you.' He said to Orly, 'I'm taking my sister.' 'Where to?' says Orly. 'We have to go down to Albany Regional Hospital. Audrey no good. She's going to die.' So me and him and Russell, I put sixty dollars in, and that took us right through to Albany. Never stopped much, only in Kojonup. Bought a little bit of a feed and water and cool drink. And we went straight through to Albany. By the time we got there it was three o'clock in the morning.

All the family was at the hospital. You should have seen the faces when we walked through that hospital door. Everybody just looked. I was like her offsider. I don't even know she was in the hospital till they said she was singing out for you to be there. I think she just wanted me to stand by her side. I think she was on her last breath then. She still knew who you were.

And they said to Audrey, 'Your favourite sister here.' And she called really softly, 'Ing, Ing.' I kept saying to her, 'You right there?' And she reckon, 'Yeah. Cold.' I said to her that I could stop talking to her with all that talk she had about not liking aeroplanes. 'Soon as I turn my back, you in the aeroplane.' Sick as she was she had a little smile there. They flew her from Perth down to Albany in the Flying Doctor aeroplane. 'See how sly you are?' She gave a little grin. She said, 'I wish I can have a laugh with you, but I'm finished now.' Even now she still makes me smile. 'Speak up a bit louder,' she says, 'I can't hear you.' And I put my hand over my heart. That was solid. I knew she understood.

Couple of days after, she was dead. That was like an empty place my heart. The saddest part was that she never told me she had cancer. She always say to me, 'That's the flu, that's only just a cold.' My brother again, I'm glad I had him. Worth all the gold in heaven. All my cousins, I felt a lot for them.

18

Special lady

WE HAVE COMPANY now in Albany – Wirlomin [Wirlomin Language and Stories Project]. I used to just sit back and let them do the talking. And those young people, they're just starting to work our language back now, which is good. I know a little bit of Noongar. Most I knew from when I was a kid. It's all sort of coming back now, but I wouldn't be able to talk it. It must be the hardest language out. My grandchildren know it and I sit back listening to them talking. If I'm talking out to family, just bits of words, but that's all. This is why I'm so disappointed in that all my life I always worked under white man's finger. I was a black white woman. They trained me that way that in my own people I didn't like their attitude and new ways of life because of being brought up in the Mission. They took all that off me. And that's what made me so shy in talking out on who I am. I just went shy. Seen everybody else talking about the wonders in their lives. I can't do that! Shame.

I was shamed even to talk out. And now I can tell people 'I'm Ing – and I'm just proud to be simply Ing.' It's solid.

That Wirlomin it's been good. Gives you a chance to get away, back home amongst your own family. Tell everyone your problems. They all got their own families. I used to be the shyest person out. You talk to me as a wadjala woman I turn my head, put head down, look away. Never say one word. This Wirlomin taught me a lot. Come a long way. Telling people where I am. I'm Ing Nellie. I'm an Elder now. My company is Wirlomin. And that gave me a sense of knowing who I was. I said to my niece, this is strange. Years ago I never used to say nothing. Just look shamed. 'Auntie Ing, you got a tongue?' I leave it up to you, I used say to Iris. You good talking. Then I started and now they sorry. Can't get me to shut up.

My little grannies they love being Wirlomin, especially little Anthony. Tell him: yeah, you Wirlomin, same as me. Best kid out when I'm around. Soon as I turn my back, 'Nanna's gone. Where she is?' Before I go I look at him and give him a look that he knows he must behave himself even when I've left. He knows that tone in my eyes. I got three little Ing's down there, they all fight over that name, Ing. I say that's my great, great grandchildren, great grandchildren. Nope, we Ing, you Nanna.

My father was a traveller; he most probably came from up the desert there somewhere. I don't know exactly which desert, must be up the other side of Kalgoorlie they reckon, more to South Australia. But everybody knew of him and they say to me, 'George Nellie your Dad?' I said, 'Yeah.' They reckon, 'Yeah, we know him.' Some old people used to come and say to me, 'We knew him. Funny man.'

And they must have sent him, them old people must have sent him down south to look for a woman. So, he must have caught the ride to Esperance. Them days it was horses, horse and cart. From Esperance he walked back towards Ravensthorpe through that thickest bush. And he had all these dogs. People give him dogs, you know, he was the sort of bloke that loved animals. And through that bush everywhere he went he killed a kangaroo with a spear, but them dogs beat him because when he got to the kangaroo it was all gone and this had been going on for nearly a week and two weeks and by then his guts was pinching.

By then he walked and walked along the beach and he couldn't walk any more, he was that hungry: too many dogs! And he got at this certain place the other side of Hopetoun; he made a fire and had a sleep. Everything he seemed to try and get, the dogs would take it off him. Right near this big cliff he went and had a good sleep, woke up, the dogs was too full. So he light a fire right around them, big circle, burned them up while they were sleep and they had nowhere to go but jump straight in the ocean.

And they reckon in the ocean, something in the ocean turned them into seals into seals and sometimes you hear like they're barking. You got a seal way of barking. They reckon the old people used to say well, that these dogs. And my Dad he told it to the old white man, Laves[9] someone, who had all the papers. And it all come out now.

Dad's story was made into a book: *Dwoort Baal Kaat*.[10] The first time I held that book in my hands I felt as if I was someone. We thought Dad was dead. And I looked at Russell and I said, 'That's powerful there. Dad never left us. He's here.' And you know, that was the strange feeling I ever had. It's a joy feeling but it's sadness. But he's alive. You know, I can feel it. It's like he says, 'That's yours. I got this far with it.' I did the paintings for that book. Painting just automatically fell into my drawing, like as if he was standing there telling me where things go.

Ever since Uncle Malcolm done what he done that time he knew Mum wanted me with her, no one ever told me a thing like that. And how I knew something was wrong when Mum and Dad was killed. That's a mystery. Her spirit came to that window above my bed at the Mission to let me know she was leaving me. I sit down and think about it myself. I still feel her beside me today, Dad too. And I'm getting them same feelings now. I can almost feel my mother again. It was like my mother never left me. Fall asleep, I know she's there. Someone sitting on the end of my bed, that's my son. I can feel my father on the side. Whether

9 Gerhardt Laves: an American linguist, the first to document Noongar language. http://www.thefreelibrary.com/Wal-Walang

10 *Dwoort Baal Kaat*. ISBN 978-1-74258-511-6 UWA Publishing 2013

this Uncle Malcolm coming out, telling me what's going to happen. Well it's here. I sense it.

Like yesterday I was on my own here sitting down having a cup of tea watching my show. All of a sudden, I got up and went into the kitchen and, 'Hey!' It was like someone sang out, 'Hey!' to me. It must have been my son, or my Dad or Mum, let me know right there, who going to come now. 'Your niece coming here directly.' There was a little noise. I know when it's my son. I say, 'I know it's you Harry.' It's like he walk out laughing at me, because you could hear the way he used walk, drag his foot. It's like he's here. Dad's the same. But yesterday was very strong. I looked around and I said to Harry John, 'Who going to come here now?' They letting me know that Kylie's halfway here, coming here. And I looked back and it was like he was telling me Kylie coming here now, my niece. But that's my family and I wouldn't want that to change forever. And about half an hour after, 'Hey, Kylie!' Little things like that. I still get it now. I don't want to get rid of that. It's been given to me by my old uncles and aunties.

I get good feelings. My surprises coming round the corner. That's never changed. I feel happy inside me and I just look at Orly even now, and I'll say, 'Look here boy, somebody coming here. Why I cleaned up this morning?' Because usually I take my time to do things. But when I get up like that and clean the house out, change the sheets and pillowcases, wash them all, get them all ready for the wash, and the place is spotless clean, dong on the door. Someone come in. 'Hey Auntie, never seen you for long time.' My nieces from south and north. I look at Orly. 'See?' And I'm happy for that. I wouldn't want to be anywhere else.

When Russell comes and sees me I'll get bang on the door. Orly will say, 'Okay Mum, who's coming?' Russell Nellie be here today or tomorrow. And next day, day after, he'll come in smiling, 'You got ten dollars on you?' Russell, my brother. Some of the times we had. We still got that bond. And I tell him I knew he'd be here, Mum told me. And he says, 'I know when you come down. She tells me down there.' And big Anthony, he knows when I'm upset.

What my old Uncle taught me back then I don't think I'll ever forget it. Uncle Malcolm said, 'You'll know one day when you get older, everything will fall into place for you.' And it's happening. I'm finding out just a little bit of what he meant by what he said. I look back now and I can see that's happening. Sixty-nine or sixty-eight and I reckon I'm receiving it. I can sense it through little things that happen around here. I could teach that good part of my life to my little grannies. I'm teaching it at the moment to my little grandson. Me and him are very close. Oh, big fella now. And he knows, he knows. I let him know. Little Anthony, he'll run to his mother and he'll say, 'My Nanny coming, my Nan be here tomorrow.' We'll pull in the next day. And that's it. I rubbed him down when he's a baby, tell him he my darmoor, darmoor. That's Wongi – my baby, my heart.

There's something there. It's different. He's like a real honest little man. He can be a devil at times. Justine, his Mum, she'll tell me afterwards, 'Ah, old girl, you too close to him. He knew you'll be here. He come and tells me a day earlier you on your way here.' It's beautiful. He's the only one who knows, and big Anthony too. I hope they'll keep that gift when they get older.

Uncle Malcolm left me with the gift of reading clouds and wind and the trees. I can read the sky. Just a little crack on the thing and somebody standing there. Next minute you see somebody coming. People you haven't seen for a long time. And I'm blessed with that. Noongar way. And say you going south and you see that cloud, just black, not moving at all. It happened to me a few times after Uncle Malcolm died. And I look at my Anthony and I say that's no good, that's wara. We're going down to something and when we get there they'll tell me somebody died. 'Oh,' he said, 'you making me feel nervous, Mum.' I say you listen to me, my baby. And when we get to where we was going, somebody dead. And Mousey, that's Anthony's nickname, he look at me and say, 'Mum, you told me that.' I tell him that you got to learn it, just the same as Uncle Malcolm used to say to me, your place to learn it. Because you're the only man in your family, only one son and you have to teach your sister that, or your grannies, your own sons.

The wind will tell you if it's going to rain or storm. But I used to watch Uncle Malcolm and Auntie Bonnie. They used to stand there, pffff. Don't know what they used to do but that wind used to come up, feel it coming. Old Albany Doctor come in, cool things down. Uncle Malcolm taught me how to do that, but I leave that to the past. As long as I know it's there on my side I know what to do.

It's powerful when I go home to Gnowangerup. Coming in from Perth way, Katanning way – it's the only way you can get into Gnowangerup – or you go through Tambellup, but I like that way because you got those old Stirling Ranges in the distance and it's all like them old people are looking, know who you are, you coming home to see us. I just sit down and have a good cry. Driving along, I say stop for a little minute, I got to stop crying. And I say thank you Mum and Dad, Uncle Malcolm. They know I'm there. All around the Stirling, you could feel it, as if all the old people are pleased you there. If you're family, you get a joy in your heart. That's lovely, top end of Borden and Gnowangerup, look at the Stirling. I know when they around. Get a warm feeling. I know they watching me. Walk anywhere. That's the most loveliest little bit I ever experienced. You know when your family there. The wind is warm, beautiful, like they telling you, 'We close now.'

I know when they don't want me doing things. I get that 'Oh no' feeling. And the older I'm getting, the more I feel connected to Noongar ways. Noongar ways is strong, very strong. Don't go anywhere. And my cousin, she's been in places where she shouldn't be. That sign will show, a sign don't go there. But this girl walked into it and they must have caught her, old Noongars. You go into there you going to get caught. Spirit too strong. Old Noongars not dead and gone. No way. They all have their eyes open, spirit eyes – and I'm proud I can see it. It's a very strong feeling. That was what Uncle Malcolm was talking about.

Might see a cloud shaped like a grave, grab a sand and chuck towards it. It will go away. That curse has gone to someone else. Me, I can do it now, but not when I was younger. Sign of history. And we go down to our old Auntie. She would have been a grand Auntie because that's my mother's Auntie. Her grave was in this farm in Ongerup. She sort of hid from them when they was shooting my family, but she saw it happen. Years ago at that river, there was an old Noongar settlement there and most of the people from Norseman and Esperance right through come there. Our family, Dabs. And this old lady was a symbol there of our family. She died of the heartache of seeing all her family dying – shot. It's a big story and I got to tell that one day. I'll get my little brother, Henry, to come with me, and Russell. And Wirlomin went down there to see where this grave was and when we was coming along, Russell reckons, 'Look up there in the front of us.' Nobody can see it. I said, 'Look up there!' Little man standing, pointing, straight down. And they said there was nothing there, only cloud. And he was showing me and Russell, you right, you going the right way. My old Uncle.

So I learnt that way and I'm still learning that way that things happening to me that's sometimes frightening, sometimes I know it's the right thing and I feel great about that. Even my old cousin say to me, 'Girl, what you got? You shining every time you come down here.' All my nieces say I'm an old powerful girl. They say, 'Auntie Ing, you got something but we don't know what it is.' I tell them I want them to know it's a gift. I'll cherish that forever. You'll know if anything happen to me. They say, 'Who give you that? Who give you those things?' No one. I watch your moorditj, I watch your faces. I get my expressions off your eyes. If you don't like me or if you are not being truthful I can see and sense that. 'How can you? We love you.'

And people who used to be more brainier than me and got on with life, they reckon, 'Ing, I don't know what's the matter with you, girl.' I say, 'I'm all right, nothing wrong with me.' They say, 'No, there's something about you. We don't know what it is but there's something.' Even my nieces come up and say to me that they know there's something there, but they don't know what it is. 'You're different to all of us.' Big Anthony, he'll look at me, 'See, they know. I can see things too,' he says. 'You taught me a lot.'

People say to me, 'Where you come from?' Oh, I'm from Albany, Gnowangerup, Borden. Pretty country. 'Oh, where that is?' 'Way down south. Go down there and have a look. Real pretty country. Nuari.' In Wongi that's pretty. That's beautiful. Nice looking.

19

Looking backward and forward

MY LITTLE SISTER, Hilary, she died when she was young. I miss her. There's only me and my brother now. He's in Katanning. He lives down there and he's got his own life. Got three kids of his own.[11] Three little grandchildren. They are so beautiful. But all of the Nellie kids, they are really handsome! I'm not showing off or anything, but they're really pretty kids. I've got three grannies here in Beechboro, all Nellies, my nephew's children. They're absolutely beautiful. And they all named after family. One's named after his first cousin, my eldest son. He's the eldest. My son's name was Harry John Nellie. This little boy's name, Harry John Nellie. Little boy named George after Dad's name, George Nellie. And little girl named Tilda Nellie after grandmother. So, they still going with us, Mum and Dad.

---

11 In the course of writing this story, one of Russell's children was killed in a motor vehicle accident. See also Afterword.

Over the years, I talk about the other girls where I come from, Gnowangerup. Half of them all went into jail because something went wrong in their lives. Young girls from then can't take it. They didn't know how to look for the good in life, even my first cousin, my sister. In and out of jail all their lives. I think, what you fellas see in jail? There's nothing there. They say, 'We got nothing to go home for. We never had Mum and Dad.' I said, 'Neither have I, you know that.' I don't want to be like that. I'd be letting Mummy down if I go and sit in prison all the time.

And that's one thing I taught myself, never go to jail. Nothing in jail. They say, 'But we not like you.' I say to them, 'You don't have to be like me. Just be yourself. You learn to pick yourself up and move on. You know, your family is your family. You be strong for them.' I often taught myself that. I taught Russell that. But Russell was one of these hard-headed people. I was always there for him when he get into trouble. Doesn't matter where he was. 'I miss you, sis.' I was always there for him. My little sister was the same. She used to call me Mum. And that to me was part of who I am today. And I'm glad I went through that. I found my family. I know where I am, who I am, where I come from. That's me! Only one Ing Nellie.

Everybody dying around me and that's a precious memory. The sad part is that when you lose someone, you stop and think. I think, oh no, look at all these young people, gone before me. I used to tell them, 'Don't feel sorry for yourself. Pick yourself up and be happy with it.' And they reckon, 'We not like you; we wish we was like you. You got your own way of doing things.' I say, 'Don't give up, your day will come. You special girl and special boy. You grow up first.' Put your arm around people and say, 'We family.' That's the only thing that keeps me going. 'You my family. I'm proud of you. Don't get down unless you really have to.'

But my nieces say, 'Auntie Ing, you can go anywhere and you got friends looking at you.' I tell them that I tell people my name, say hello, it's a beautiful day. People say to me, 'You look happy today.' Little incidents like that. Even now, I can talk to any people. And they all say, 'Why do you say hello?' I said, 'That's just me. That's how I been brought up.' The girls come over and say hello to me. And I was at the shopping centre and this African woman, one was in a wheelchair. She just said, 'Hello dear.' Well, me and her friends now, but she got a funny name; I couldn't pronounce it. We friends. I said, 'You are my best mate.' She thought it was great. Oh, we stand and have a good yarn as if we've known each other for a lifetime. My gang walk past and they say, 'You don't know them people.' I tell them, 'Yeah, I know her, she's my friend.' 'We can't be like that, Auntie, that's shame!' It's not shame. Those fellows taught me how to use my tongue. I was the frighteningest fella out there, but something clicked. Someone must have untied my tongue here somewhere.

I'm thankful that I come all the way for me to be there. Someone must be keeping me busy, because most of the people in my age have all died – can't face life. I was like that myself when I was drinking. But what for? It's a different feeling now. I just can't stand the stuff. So I said to myself, sometime I let myself go. I want to let people know who Ing is, that's what I want more in life, just simply being Ing, thankful Ing, through all the ups and downs in life. That's a part of my life that has made me stronger – in my right mind for a change.

A lot of young people down home, half of them are all six foot under. Younger than me! Life is impossible for them to live. Drugs and alcohol the killer of them poor fellas. That's the sad part of it. I think, where they going? What happened to them? Poor little things. When they go through hard time, they come up and see me. I tried talking to them. That's all you can do. They don't like preaching. It's their life. They all grown up now and got big heads. They've got to do it themselves. I been there myself. I was a terrible drunk. All the ups and downs in life, nowhere to go and being a street kid. When you on the streets you sit back, have a drink, and one lead to another. Next thing you fighting the biggest bloke there, or the biggest woman, even though you get a hiding. Ah, true, it was a funny time. Monkey's cage I call those years. Ah, when you sick of fighting you jump in the water, Swan River. Swim around like sharks – until you see one. Gave up when I got pregnant with Harry and they took me to Mogumber. Afterwards, I travelled. Enjoyed a good drink when I had one, but moved on. Always had a job to go to. I never sat around, sitting down doing nothing. Couple of times I might of. But from that time I really looked after myself. Thought I did. Went home to Albany. Well, I hit the drink again. But I didn't want to be like that, so I gave it up. I don't mind a little beer now and then. It's good! Good for the system, isn't it?

Kids nowadays they just never had the strength to stand up for themselves and say, right, I want to be on my own. It's sad. That's why I feel so sad for my family. I love them all, each and every one of them. But to see young kids go down like that through this gunja and drinking around, you know, that makes me feel no good. I've seen too many lives go down. Back in the 60s, young kids just finished school and they hit that drink. Didn't know much about gunja. Weren't there then. Only in the late 60s it come out properly. You know, beer was okay. Then they sold wine and Tawny Port. That was like watermelon wine. And to see how many little kids from nappies and then into that drink. A lot of kids all dead now. All died very, very young. Beautiful, pretty kids from south. Kids you change their nappies, cuddle them. That's when I started thinking, I'm going to stop this. This is not for me. And I'm glad I done that.

I had a girl rang me the other day. She's in hospital and she's going through a terrible time in life. And this little girl, I used to look after her because her mother was a terrible drug addict. She said, 'Mum Helen, you're the only one I could talk to.' And it hit me on the heart, you know? And I'm thinking oh dear. She's stuck in this place. My heart went out to her and I said, 'Never forget who you are, baby. And you know we can't do anything for you out here. It's against their rules. Have a little prayer,' I said to her. 'I love you, I'll always love you. You can always ring up and say Hello Auntie.' And she was crying, 'I want to get out.'

But they told us after we can't do nothing, it's up to her mother. And I said to her, 'You have to try and pull your side of the bargain if you want help. I'll be waiting there for you if you decide you don't want to live there. That's your decision. They told me I can't do nothing. I'm telling you this from my heart.' And she rang me up again and she said, 'Old girl, you are a big lady. You're beautiful.' And I felt like I'd done something good. And I said, 'I love you. Don't ever forget that. You know where I live when you come out, you welcome home. My doors be open to you.' She couldn't talk. I couldn't talk. She said, 'I'm sorry for making you cry, Old Mum. I'm going to try and get myself out of here. Tell Mousey I love him.' I did and he said, 'Mum, you're a big woman. You're powerful.' And that's made me feel good – so good. Thinking of it I feel like having a tear in my eye.

One of my cousins she had one daughter, and to me she was my angel. Doesn't matter where I was she will always come and see me. When they showed me the newspaper, mother came and told me. Accident coming back from Northam or something. Truck hit that car, killed her. She was driving. I said, 'No, not my angel.' And that really hurt me. That was in the early 70s I think. I got a photo. She's beautiful. Only one little daughter they had and she's gone. And that's another sad part of my life. I get so caring and loving people, getting close to them and they gone.

All the younger girls that are younger than me, they look older than me. They grew up in the 70s, that's when gunja started then. Back then we didn't know how bad that was. I think we was lucky for that. And all hard drugs that was around and that. And half of them little kids that was just finishing school was already on this stuff. Now they look older than us, but they've got beautiful kids.

Now things are older and wiser and I look around and I see a lot of Noongar girls nowadays never really give thoughts to their mothers and fathers, you know. Lives is too fast. Their fathers and mothers still going, but they rather leave them there, let them go along. They got people looking after them and I think how sad. I say, 'Don't get upset with your Mum and Dad. That's all your life there. You come from them. I wish I had my Mum and Dad.' And you wouldn't see me like that. I'd have been right with them now I wouldn't allow them go into an old people's home. Not while I can do things for them. I'd look after my Mum and Dad. They brought me into this world. But we never been blessed with a Mum and Dad through growing up.

I'd see all these younger kids grow up, growing into teenage life and they tell me how much they hated their Mum and their Dad, and I feel really sad for them. 'You lucky you got a Mum and Dad. I never had that, me and Russell and Hilary. I had to look after my little brother and sister. It's my job. Don't talk to me about hating your Mum and Dad.' I seen little grannies throw things at their Mum and Dad and that. My gang, I just point my finger. You do what you're told or you get smack. They know that finger.

Lot of the girls now, kids I've known since they were babies, they say, 'Auntie, we can't make it. We don't know how to get faith in life.' Them Noongars down there, they need something to encourage them to put their faith in something, get us all close together. We family, we need each other. The girls come up and say to me, 'You know, Auntie, you powerful old lady, boss old lady. We all love you.' 'And I love you all too,' I say. 'Give me a big cuddle, because that's what you need, a cuddle. I never had that from Mum and Dad because they was dead. It's my place to give you a cuddle.'

I seen a lot of things happen, too, in the bush with these girls that say wrong things against old people. One girl, she even told lies about her father. And that made me stop and think. 'Come on!' I said. 'Come on, your father never done that. Your father was a shepherd. That's why I just want to get well away from you. I want no part of that. I love my old people and I live my life knowing that they are with me all the time. Don't tell lies about it.'

I know Noongar way and Christian way, too. I know both sides of the stories. So, I never used to worry about it. I was brought up that way. They talking right when it comes to the good old gospel. Tell everybody I'm a bush Baptist. I can't stand Jehovah Witnesses. Catholics are the worst offenders out for me. But I get by with it. I got lots of Catholic friends.

But them Mormons! When I was in Kalgoorlie, they were door-knocking on their bikes, so we went along just to see what this church is all about. We didn't know nothing about it. People said if we go there you be married to one of them. They allowed to have any ladies from all over the world in that church. We ended up going to it. They put us right in the front. Never again! I didn't know what they was talking about. I giggled all the way because they talking about that prophet man. How come he's a prophet? I got up in the end and I said, 'Look brothers, I love you, thank you for that, but I'm a bush Baptist, that's not my beliefs, now where's the door?' I couldn't get through that door quick enough. Cheek of him. They reckon they going to marry us. I was frightened they might say, 'I want you to be my bride.' I'm thinking no way, not this Noongar and walked out. Terrible. They do that, eh? They can have as many wives as they like? No way! This Noongar would have torn the door down. It's like a heathen church, like that other one, Psychology or Scientology. Weird. Bush Baptist, you can understand them. I'm old bush Baptist and I'm proud to be bush Baptist, brought up on the Holy

Bible. That Bible through the years has brought me through a lot of rough places.

Looking back now, Kalgoorlie was a funny side in my life. Good time. I was overjoyed to be there. They taught me a lot, Wongi way. Bit of a cheeky person at times, but that's natural when you young. You don't get into an argument with everybody, eh? Knew all the girls by the time I left Kal. I had a good 30–35 years up there, working in pubs, working in dining rooms, in hostels. Everybody knew me. Old Wongi they knew that. They call me widebella, whitefella. I call out Wiyartu, gone, that's me. I'm Noongar. Yeah, but they was good days, fun days, they were the fun days and we had good times. Times now me and the girls from Kalgoorlie can sit down. Didja, sister, they say to me, Wongi way, 'You my didja, we adopt you. You sister. Miss you, sister. Ngarlang.' That's Noongar – drink. Pull sad faces. I go don't pull face at me. 'Kuwarra, kuwarra, sit down, sit down. We tell you, don't be Noongar all your life.' I say, well I am, aren't I? Wiyartu. I love the Wongi language. Noongar's the hardest language I ever spoken. I still don't even know it, only little odds and ends that we grew up with. I love old Wongi.

Telling my story gives me comfort. See, this is what I want to get out of me so I can be myself and I want this to happen. There's a few more tears, but I'll come across them down the road. I'm still searching for my answers. And that's why I'm so close to my brother. Oh, we have some ding-dong arguments even now. I don't let him bluff me around and he don't let me bluff him around. No one don't want to be in the middle of it. Wife usually go on down the road, her and the kids. We sit back, have a good fight. But he's right. When he come to his senses he says, 'That's my big Mum there.' That's the hurting part. All through life, I didn't have a tear for a long time but at the moment, with everything going on around me it just automatically comes. A little bit of tear wouldn't hurt.

I don't know what my life would be like if things was different, if I wasn't in the Mission. I might have been one of those old ladies now, worrying about the kids. I might have had about a multitude of kids, don't know what they doing. I tell you I been blessed in how I been brought up. I been blessed. Only little part of it they gave me. Or I reckon I might have been one of the oldest drunks out now. Fight with all the girls on the streets. You know, cheeky old woman I would be.

Drink nearly killed me. Listening to everybody, get in with the crowd, Albany. Albany main place. Them young girls when they want to go out and look for boyfriend, 'Oh, come along with us, Auntie Ing. You the main one. We'll stick right with you.' Look for them years later, they come along with half a dozen kids. 'You can look after them for us, ana?' 'No, thank you, that's your responsibility. Go away, you kids,' I'll say to them. 'What are you going to do with all your children?' That's sad.

You know, that was them days. Most of everybody now

from my days, white people and all, dead. Very young age. That's what I couldn't understand in life. And they lived to a certain age and then something happen and they're dead. My gang always say to me, 'How old you, Ing?' 'I'm 68, 69 this birthday.' 'No you're not.' Even now, they say to me, 'No you're not, you're only in your 50s.' Gah, in a way I wish I was. I never got a birth certificate. Don't know if there ever was one, being born on the reserve. I got the form for them to look and see if there ever was one. But my Welfare documents say my birthday is July 18, 1947. Come to think of that, I think going in the mission they put that on as my birthday, but really, no one know my birthday. I don't feel that age; I feel younger.

What really made me hurt was that they said I wasn't entitled to nothing of that Stolen Generations[12] compensation. Thousands of people got that. Not me. They don't believe me. It's not right. I go plenty of times these Noongar in offices and I say I'm Helen Nellie, this is me. I was a State Ward when I was six or nine year old. Grew up in Gnowangerup Mission. And they tell me I can't get no credit for stolen generation. And I got my history here. It's there

12 Stolen Generations: Between 1910–1970, large numbers of Australian Aboriginal and Torres Strait Islander children were removed from their parents or extended family by means of force, intimidation or coercion, ostensibly to protect the child from neglect or destitution. These children were placed in Christian missions or white foster homes and were denied their Aboriginality.

on paper, all those documents and you just couldn't seem to do nothing.

Now I'm thinking I can do it. I can get what I'm looking for. I'm a bit older now, realise what life's all about. There's part of me that's gone and part of me that's still here. I'm part of this beautiful country. It makes me cry when I look at the documents. I cry every time I read them. That's all my history on Native Welfare. They took me away from my Mum and Dad – twice. Time they give me something instead. Even now, kids that never been in the Mission getting thousands of dollars. This needs to be pushed. I know two boys brought up in the reserve. Never even been in the Mission. They got four thousand and here I'm screaming for money. All them years in the Mission.

I'm at that age now I can see how my old people used to live. Like they had their own way of life. They keep it, that's theirs. And I'm proud of that because I had a little part of it. That was the best part of my growing up and finding out who I am. When that truck came and I went into the Mission, yeah, I was excited with the excitement of the other kids. 'Come Auntie, come for ride.' Stand there. For years I used to stand there, look around, see who coming up the road, see who going to tell me something. My Mum and Dad around? And that's the part in my life now I'm starting to feel it. All that time I had my name taken off me, had to learn one way of life. 'Forget that old life. It doesn't belong to you anymore.' And way back, I can remember thinking why people do that. And I think there's a little bit of hurt still there in my heart and that's something I will never, ever get used to. As long as life will take, that's something I will keep in my memory.

In Borden and the Stirling Ranges it's like those old people there are looking and can see right through you coming in, and that touches my heart. You know they're there. Okay Mum, I'm coming home. Tears automatically come every time I go home. The memories are there. That's a time I got a feeling my old people are with me. It's your place to tell who you are. And it's almost like I'm looking back at them and saying what I got to say now. I say to Orly, 'You lucky, you don't hear things, but I can.' I know when I'm doing the right thing, I'm happy. So it's my place now to tell you this story, because I been there. Didn't like it, but I had to live it. And all them precious years of Mum and Dad dying on me. That was the hardest part of my growing up, away from Mum and Dad. I never lost that love. I kept it in my heart. That's why I'm always listening to someone and their problems. People bring their problems here and they feel good after they go. I think that must have been Mum helping me somewhere along the line.

I learnt a lot over the years and I teach my grannies now, in Albany. They're my little rocks, especially little Anthony; he's so much like his Dad. He's got pretty little eyes. And you know when he's getting into trouble because he give me that funny look and I put my one finger up and point at him. 'Not me, Nan,' he'll say and point to another grandson. 'Not me, Nan.' He knows before time when I'm coming to see him. Special. That's something I'd just love to tell the world about. He's very strong that way. Must be this old woman called Ing I reckon.

The Dreamtime, it'll always be there for me. You can pick out any stories you like, to tell. They're so real – stories that have been passed down through the years. It's up to us to keep them going. I tell my grannies that. You gotta keep it going one day. That's Dreamtime. That's the beauty of where you are. My kids, they say, 'Tell us that story again, Nan.' And they have a good laugh about it. I tell them, listen, it's your turn soon to tell that same story to your kids. They reckon, 'Yeah, I will, I will.' Fast little minds. They can either go one way or the other and I wish I stay alive until that happens. Guide them through life so they know who they are, who they belong to. That would make me so happy. Let's be proud of something in life. We had everything else taken off us.

And it's too lovely, the little grannies. They're the greatest joy. They set you free, too. Make you smile and enjoy life. I got half a dozen little ones, they all Ing too. I'm Nanny. There's only one Ing and that's Nanna. 'Nup, you Nanna. I'm Ing.' You not Ing, you little wadjala girl. 'Nah, nah!' She don't like it. She's fair. Golden hair, very pretty. But loves me. She's a big girl now. She goes to kinder-garten. I sit next to her and I say Ing, ah you deadly girl, and she laughs. But that's part of where I come from. And I wouldn't change it for the world.

My future, that's a mystery. I feel great, really great. I feel good inside me. What I can see in my future is these things here, home, looking after my pretty old man. Husband who eat all my chocolate and Rice Cream. I've got nothing to complain about, eh? I think I'm pretty settled now. It doesn't matter what I do in life, I'll always do it for a little while, then I'm off, gone, looking out for new horizons. Got to be something over there somewhere. Just be myself. I'm here for my brother, my nieces and nephews. When everyone want a shoulder to cry on, I'll be there. I know I'm old but I'm in my prime. I just love where I am this time in my life. Just being thankful for a smile, looking out my little window and looking at the trees and the blue sky. I wouldn't want to be anywhere else but there, right where I am now. I love it.

Afterword

I USED TO look at people who write books and I thinking one day I'm going to do that. I don't know how, but I'll do that. This book has topped everything off for me because I told my story. I know some of it is strong. It's meant to be. I'm a proud Nanny, the oldest from up north and down south, too. There's only me and my brother down there. Odd nephew and nieces, but I'm the oldest out of the whole lot of Nellies. And I like to show people that part of my life. I'm able to conquer anything if I put my mind to it. To let people know I'm just simply Ing. I wouldn't want to be anyone else.

RIP Russell Nellie – June 2017

Over the last couple of years, Russell, he was changing. Sugar, I think. One time he couldn't talk. He was forever up here in hospital, Fiona Stanley. He'd kick up for a smoke. He weren't allowed to smoke, but he used to get away with it. But he'd get well and go home to his family in Katanning.

I don't know what happened, but one night only a little while ago I was lying back; restless sleep this night. I couldn't even sleep properly. I look at the window and I just see as if something was telling me something. Twelve o'clock the phone rang. Russell's wife Theresa rang me up, told me he went to sleep and they can't wake him up, revive him. I was shocked. It was just like as everything just hit me right in the face. I couldn't speak to even tell my husband what was going on. After about an hour she rang back again, told me he's gone. It left me speechless. I couldn't even find the words to say that my little brother's gone. I tried talking but nothing. He was gone. He's not coming back this time.

Looking back on all the years of looking at him growing up, things he used to say to me, we used to sit back and have a cruel laugh. Russell was the one that had the brains in our family. He was going to be a teacher. His heart was set on being a teacher.

Russell was the only brother I loved, my little baby brother. I miss him so much in my life.

But, he left me with a voice and precious memories of who he was. He was my little shining star and I'll treasure that until another day come and Mum and Dad take me home. Treasured memories of my little brother, Tow Tow. You're always in my heart, buddy. We'll always be there together. Always. Forever.

Appendix: The Ravensthorpe Massacre

From Wikipedia:

Koora (1880) Noongar John Dunn wadam. Yandawalla baal nitja nyininy, Dartaban baal nitja nyininy. Noongar wadjela baalap bakitj. Wadjela manatj-Dunn-moort waangk: Yandawala Dunn kitj-baaminy. Dunn noytj.

Birdiya wadjela-'judge' waangk: Yoowart Yandawalla Dunn wadam.

Boorda, Cocanarup-ak, boola boola Noongar noytj. Dunn moort baalap waadam, ('rifle')-baaminy.

Nitja 'plaque' bokitja Cocanarup waangk:

The 1913 plaque reads in full:

Narkel Nanap nitja dwonk-kaditjiny. Ngalak demanga nitja nyininy kwel mia waanginy waaliny

waalanginy. Ngalakat Noongar koora koorliny
yey, kaarlak koorliny, boojar waalbrininy

This area of country has a harsh, complex and sometimes contradictory history. Many Noongar people were killed here, and all that death and the apartheid-like 20th century legislation meant many of our families were never able to return and reconcile themselves to what had happened.

But Noongar people were the first to create human community here and, in different ways, helped build our modern society. Noongar people have been guides and workers, warriors and midwives, dancers and diplomats. We believe all of us grow from our birth grounds, our histories and the quality of our human relationships.

Bardlanginy doinj-doinj Noongarang wadjela kediny. Yey Nyoondok nitja nyininy. Now you are here. Listen. Breathe.

The region of Kukenarup, or Cocanarup in English, is infamous for the sustained massacre of many Noongar (up to 30 men, women and children, in another source over 30) at various times after 1880. These random killings were in revenge for the lawful killing in 1880 of the settler John Dunn for raping a 13 year old Noongar girl. John Dunn was the son of the Ravensthorpe pastoralist James Richard Dunn, who with his five sons and daughter had started sheep farming at the property in 1871, after taking out a pastoral lease in 1868. The Dunn's were founding settlers in the area. The massacre is variously called the Cocanarup Massacre after the name of the homestead, the Ravensthorpe Massacre after the nearest local town, or the Kukenarup Massacre. John Dunn was speared by Yandawalla and others for his crime, in accordance with Noongar law. Yandawalla (or Yandawulla or Yungala) was arrested and charged with the murder of John Dunn in accordance with Wadjela law. Dartaban (Dartemera, also known as 'Jumbo') was also involved, and was a witness in the trial of Yandawalla (1881). Yandawalla was acquitted of the murder; from the South Australian Register of 26 November 1881:

> The native Yangala, tried recently for the murder of Mr. John Dunn, has been acquitted owing to the unsatisfactory manner in which the evidence of the black witness was interpreted.

Reprisal killings of a number of Noongar occurred, both prior to and for some time following the acquittal. All these killings are called the Kukenarup Massacre, although genocide would be a more accurate term due to the sustained nature of the events. It is sad that too many Wadjela histories of the area either ignore the massacre completely, or gloss over it and concentrate on the execution of the child rapist John Dunn rather than the many Noongar killed in reprisal for his death.

A memorial to the historical incident was opened in May 2015 in the region. There is a plaque, display board and boards along a walk trail with quotes from various Noongar community members and families at the Cocanarup Memorial, approximately 15 kilometres West of Ravensthorpe. The memorial text was written by Kim Scott, a Wirlomin Noongar man.

John Dunn's grave is at Cocanarup Homestead. The ruined homestead is visible from the memorial site.

Glossary and notes

ana?

question (Wirlomin Language and Stories Project). Also unna in other languages.

balyat

1. little creature that looks like a person, cheeky and mischievous with magical powers (Whitehurst)
2. The little people (Douglas)
3. Spirit of the echo (Bindon and Chadwick)

Ing uses the word in Ch.6 to describe a cloud shaped like a grave, a sign of death. In her Noongar dictionary, Rose Whitehurst uses the word 'birnt' for a death cloud.

Bandyup

women's prison in metropolitan Perth

bany

pigface, *Carpobrotus* sp. Succulent coastal native groundcover. Alternate spelling paing.

bardi

edible, high protein wood-eating larvae found in root systems and under the bark of certain trees.

https://en.wikipedia.org/wiki/Witchetty_grub

bobtail

see yoorn

boodjari

pregnant (Douglas). Alternative spelling poojarri (Bindon and Chadwick).

bream

edible fish species

bungarra (Wongi), kardar (Noongar) alternative spelling karrda

Large goanna also known as Racehorse Goanna, *Varanus gouldii*

https://en.wikipedia.org/wiki/Sand_goanna

Carrolup

Opened in 1913 as a reserve/settlement for the Noongar people from the Katanning area. Closed in 1922, it was reopened in 1938. It became the Marribank Baptist Mission in 1952 and operated until 1970.

chook

colloquialism for chicken

Claremont Mental Hospital

at the time Western Australia's largest psychiatric hospital

damper

unleavened bread made from flour, salt and water, baked in the coals

darmoor (Noongar and Wongi)

grandfather. Also baby or small child.

Same term used for grandchildren and grandparents or others in need of special nurturing. Both dear to the heart and need to be cared for. Continuum of life.

didja

sister

Aboriginal pronunciation or accent for the English word sister.

djanak

devil, evil spirit (Douglas, Whitehurst)

djilki

gilgie freshwater crayfish

http://www.fish.wa.gov.au/Documents/recreational_fishing/fact_sheets/fact_sheet_freshwater_crayfish.pdf

dolphin

bottlenose dolphin *Tursiops truncatus*, coastal bottlenose (Indo-Pacific) dolphin *Tursiops aduncus*, common dolphin *Delphinus delphis*, dusky dolphin *Lagenorhynchus obscurus*, and Risso's dolphin *Grampus griseus*, can be located in coastal waters in Australia's southwest.

gunja

marijuana

hangi

traditional New Zealand Maori method of cooking on hot rocks in a pit

herring

Arripis georgianus

ing

spoilt

jarrah

eucalyptus marginata

https://en.wikipedia.org/wiki/Eucalyptus_marginata

johnnycake

small, flat bread made from flour and water, cooked over coals

Traditionally, Noongar people would have used crushed seeds, such as from acacias or zamia seeds, the latter being highly neurotoxic if not carefully prepared in a time-honoured way.

kaanya (Whitehurst), karnyya (Bindon and Chadwick)

shame, shy, embarrassed

The word 'shame' has a different meaning in Aboriginal English, indicating shyness or embarrassment. In this context, Ing means that Russell's behaviour was an embarrassment to the family.

kaat wara

mentally unstable or unwell. Also used for someone acting silly.

karrda

goanna, see bungarra

kooding (Wirlomin Language and Stories Project)

carrot, grows in the ground, purple in colour, red when ripe. Very hot when raw. Cook on coals or in hot ashes. Alternative spelling koordinm, kwardiny (Whitehurst). Koordyn (Bindon and Chadwick).

koomak (Wirlomin Language and Stories Project)

little green berry. Same as cummock coorrup, cooroop, koorep, koorap, kooroop. Berry, sweet fruit shaped like a cucumber, grows on a vine. Can be eaten all year round. (Whitehurst, Bindon and Chadwick)

Koongamia

suburb of Perth, derived from the Noongar word 'koongkamaya' meaning a hut on the shoulder of a hill

koordany

shy; without shame

Ing uses the word as 'I'm looking at you,' to give a non-verbal warning to modify behaviour. (Whitehurst)

kornt (Wirlomin Language and Stories Project)

camp or shelter. Alternative spelling kwarnt, koornt or kwont.

kurtas
brothers (Noongar, Wongi and others)

kuwarra
sit down, wait until I've finished (Wongi)

kwandang (Wirlomin Language and Stories Project)
wild cherry. Wild peach. Alternative spelling quandong, kwondong.

kwardiny
wild carrot (grows in the ground, purple in colour, red when ripe, very hot raw, cook on coals or in hot ashes) (Whitehurst).

Lore, Lore man

Some make a distinction between Lore (the body of knowledge held by all of the people) and Law (for the elders who dispense the Law). In this book, Lore is used throughout.

mal (Wirlomin Language and Stories Project)
small green berry on prickly groundcover. Alternative spelling mull. (Bindon and Chadwick)

mallee
dwarf eucalyptus, widespread throughout the dry, inland areas of Australia. The gnarled, disproportionately large roots are used as firewood or rustic furniture.

maran

anglicised locally to marron. Freshwater crayfish endemic to Western Australia. A decapod crustacean, possessing ten legs.

http://www.fish.wa.gov.au/Species/Marron

marloo

red kangaroo (Whitehorse)

mia mia

hut, shelter

moorditj

1. good, strong (Whitehurst)

Ing describes being able to discern a person's integrity – or lack of – by looking into their face, seeing their moorditj.

2. Medicine man (Douglas)

mungart

jam gum, sweet gum, sugar gum, *Acacia acuminate*

The mungart tree symbolises the strength and survival of the Noongar people. It is cited in Bills presented to the Western Australian Parliament which led to the Noongar Recognition Act, 2016.

ngarlang

drink

Wilf Douglas specifies ngarlang as drinking wine.

nookert

sleep (Wirlomin Language and Stories Project and Whitehurst)

Noongar

Aboriginal person from the southwest of Western Australia. Various spellings. Noongar, Nyungar, Nyoongar, Nyoongah.

nuari

pretty or beautiful (Wongi)

Pooya

a nickname used by Ing's mother for her father

quardiny

bush medicine

rouseabout

unskilled labourer

salmon

West Australian salmon, *Arripis truttaceus*

skippy

skipjack, silver trevally, *Pseudocaranx georgianus*

shanghai

crudely made slingshot

Word commonly used throughout Australia and New Zealand.

Stirling Ranges

https://parks.dpaw.wa.gov.au/park/stirling-range

tailor

Pomatomus saltatrix

tiger

tiger snake, *Notechis scutatus,*the sixth most venomous in the world

https://australianmuseum.net.au/tiger-snake

wadjala

non-Aboriginal (Wirlomin Language and Stories Project and Douglas). Alternative spelling wadjela.

wara

bad (Whitehurst). No good. Sick. Alternative spelling warra.

wati

stick (Wongi)

weelo

bush stone curlew, *Burhinus grallarius.* A nocturnal, ground-dwelling bird with an eerie, high-pitched call, often heard in chorus with others.

http://www.birdlife.org.au/bird-profile/bush-stone-curlew?_ga=1.171074528.1907458922.1486392496

wetj

emu (Wirlomin Language and Stories Project). Alternative spelling waitj (Whitehurst).

Ing's family totem

wiya

no

wiyartu

nothing (Wongi)

woka

a cover. Roof or blanket (Douglas).

Covering made from jute bag. Can be used to make a shelter. Also used as a blanket (Whitehurst). Alternative spelling wagger, wagga.

Wongi

Aboriginal people of the western desert and goldfields of Western Australia.

Wooroloo

minimum security prison on the outskirts of Perth

yongka

kangaroo (Wirlomin Language and Stories Project, Whitehurst, Douglas). Alternative spelling yongher, yonger, yonker, yongor {m}, war {f} (Bindon and Chadwick)

yoorn (Noongar)

bobtail skink *Tiliqua rugosa rugosa.*

https://en.wikipedia.org/wiki/Tiliqua_rugosa

yowa

hello (Wongi)

yo-yo

dancing/bouncing around the boxing ring with short, random steps so that his opponent was unable to gauge where he was going to be next. That way he could take his opponent by surprise.

References

Bindon, Peter and Chadwick, Ross, *A Nyoongar Wordlist: from the south-west of Western Australia*, 2nd edition, 2011

Douglas, Wilf, *Illustrated dictionary of the South-West Aboriginal language.* Claremont, Australia: Edith Cowan University, 1996

Whitehurst, Rose, *Noongar Dictionary*, second edition 1997

Wirlomin Language and Stories Project wordlist. Wirlomin Noongar Language & Stories Project. http://Wirlomin.com.au/